SECRET AGENT

A MEMOIR

SANDY CATHCART

Visit Needle Rock Press at www.needlerockpress.com
Visit the author's website at **www.scatsandycathcart.com**

SECRET AGENT: A Memoir is a work of nonfiction
Some names and identifying details
have been changed to protect certain individuals.
Copyright © 2022 Sandy Cathcart

Cover design by Sandy Cathcart Copyright © 2022 Sandy Cathcart
Photo of Sandy and Jeff (pg. 270) by Ronald Rushton
Photo of Cat and Sandy (pg. 246) by Pictures by Julie

All rights reserved. No portion of this book may be reproduced, stored in a retrieval system, or transmitted in any form or by any means—electronic, mechanical, photocopy, recording, scanning, or other—except for brief quotations in critical reviews or articles, without the prior written permission of the publisher.

Scripture quotations (unless otherwise specified) are taken from the Holy Bible, New International Version®, NIV® Copyright ©1973, 1978, 1984, 2011 by Biblica, Inc.® Used by permission. All rights reserved worldwide.

Scripture quotations marked TPT are from The Passion Translation®. Copyright © 2017, 2018, 2020 by Passion & Fire Ministries, Inc. Used by permission. All rights reserved. ThePassionTranslation.com.

Published in the United States by Needle Rock Press
341 Flounce Rock Rd.
Prospect, OR 97536

Needle Rock Press books may be purchased in bulk for ministry purposes by contacting sandycathcart@gmail.com.

ISBN-13: 978-1-943500-22-2 (paperback)
ISBN: 978-1-943500-23-9 (ebook)

To Cat

Our love will only grow stronger in eternity.

INTRODUCTION

> The righteous will flourish like a palm tree,
> they will grow like a cedar of Lebanon;
> planted in the house of the LORD,
> they will flourish in the courts of our God.
> They will still bear fruit in old age,
> they will stay fresh and green,
> proclaiming, "The Lord is upright;
> he is my Rock, and there is no wickedness in him.
> —*Psalm 92:12-15*

A dear friend calls me her "Secret Agent Woman." I always cringe a little at that, because I know what she means. I don't look like much, but God does amazing things through me. That should be enough, right? But the pride and humanness in me want to look good.

And that's the crux, isn't it? No matter how much we try to die to ourselves, there's always a part of us that sneaks up to grab attention. Look at me! Aren't I something? And as fast as it sneaks up, we feel ashamed, and then we sink to the depths thinking we couldn't possibly be used by God at all.

In times like these, I put on a worship playlist, open my Bible, and remind myself of what is true and good and lovely. God loves me! Not because I'm an amazing Secret Agent Woman, but because He made me just the way I am, and I have become His faithful daughter. Even that, I didn't do in my own strength. He filled me with His Holy Spirit and teaches me daily how to walk with Him.

This is an amazing way to live, and I've been doing it for more than forty years. So now, I want to share with you how I've seen God at work in the sunny, mountain-top seasons as well as in the deep-in-the-pit seasons.

It is my hope that something in these pages will plant a seed of hope in you that will grow into a magnificent tree. God has promised we will be standing trees, bearing fruit well into old age, if we simply continue to put our trust in Him.

I am a faithful daughter, not because I do everything right, but because I turn back to God each and every time I fall. Dear friend, you can do the same.

We are still green trees!

CONTENTS

Introduction	....	v
1.	Broken	1
2.	Friend of God	15
3.	Kindness	25
4.	Blessing	35
5.	Listening	47
6.	Think	61
7.	Wonder	75
8.	Faith	89
9.	Breathe	103
10.	Crossing Borders	117
11.	Ancient Paths	133
12.	Love Song	145
13.	Lost	159
14.	Restoration	171
15.	Chosen	187
16.	Tracks	201
17.	Awake	217
18.	Heart Check	235
19.	Creator Redeemer	247
	The Song	271
	Take the Secret Agent Quiz	274
	Acknowledgments	275
	About the Author	276
	Contact	278

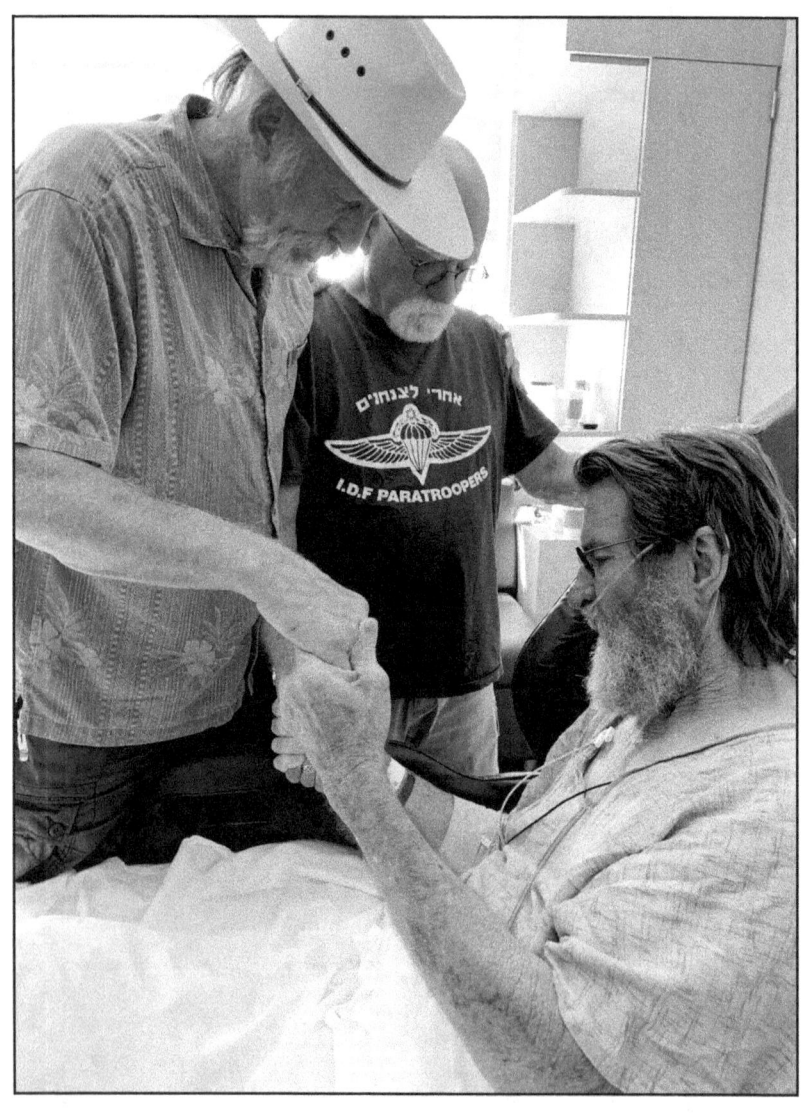

Cat's hunting buddies,
Jean Paul Di Betta and Nick Lazzareschi,
praying for him in the hospital.

1
BROKEN

> My spirit is broken,
> my days are cut short,
> the grave awaits me.
>
> —*Job 17:1*

Portland International Airport
October 23, 2017

WE STOOD IN LINE TO BOARD OUR PLANE when my phone rang. I saw the call was from my husband, so I answered.

"The doctor wants you there before she will tell me anything," Cat said.

His words made me drop my bag and stop.

My daughter Michelle kept moving forward before she realized I had stayed behind. "Mom?"

I couldn't muster a word.

We were expecting the results of a scan of Cat's head, but neither of us thought it would be anything too bad. Cat was healthy and strong. He was simply having trouble finding his words.

The news must be really bad if the doctor wants me there.

"Mom?" my daughter said again.

People began pulling their bags around me.

"I need to come home," I told Cat.

"No," he said. "I made an appointment for the day you return."

Tears flooded down my face. How could I possibly get on a plane headed for Disneyland while wondering what was wrong with the most important person in my life?

"Branden has been looking forward to this for two years," Cat said. "Go and have a good time."

The trip was a gift for our grandson Branden's graduation. I had taken two years to save the money. If we didn't go now, it would never happen.

We boarded the plane. I sat in silence, praying, begging God to heal my husband and give me peace and help me to trust He had everything under control. I wondered if Cat had some kind of brain tumor. Surely, whatever was wrong with Cat was something doctors could operate on and make him all better again.

When my family landed and boarded a shuttle in Los Angeles, a woman sat across from me looking as if she carried the weight of the world on her shoulders.

"Is this your first time in LA?" I asked.

"No," she said. "This used to be my home. I'm returning to help my dying son."

With that statement, we were immediately connected.

The rest of the ride, we shared our breaking hearts and prayed together, then I gave her a signed copy of my book, *Wild Woman: A Daughter's Search for a Father's Love*, with a promise to continue to pray.

Remembering to pray for others is easy when your own heart is breaking. You simply include them when you're praying for your own needs. I included her and her son in all my prayers during the next ten days while we visited all the popular places in LA.

God was gracious to give me peace. I was thankful for that precious time with my daughter and grandkids.

When we returned to Portland, I said goodbye to my daughter and grandkids. Then I hopped in my car and drove alone 400 miles to the White City VA Medical Center. I met Cat in the parking lot, and we walked in together.

A nurse led us to an exam room where she seated us in front of a video screen to wait for our teleconference. It was my first experience visiting a doctor who was several hundred miles away. The doctor wasted no time in telling us the grim news.

"Your husband has severe white matter disease," she said. "There is nothing we can do."

I stared straight ahead, feeling my throat tighten and tears starting to well. I didn't dare look at Cat. We already were holding hands. Each of us tightened our grip.

"I don't understand," I finally said.

She explained that Cat probably had Alzheimer's and would progressively worsen.

"Don't put anything off," she said. "Whatever you've been wanting to do together, you need to do."

"Surely, there is something—"

She shook her head, saying nothing.

I let go of Cat's hand and grabbed a Kleenex box. Nothing could stop my tears. Cat held me while I wished I could be stronger. He had been there for me for forty-seven years. Now I needed to be there for him. Instead, I was falling apart.

We each had an hour's drive in front of us. I told Cat I would stop and give our kids the news, and then I would meet him at home.

Nothing seemed real. *How could this have happened to such a dynamic man?*

By the time I reached Ashland, I couldn't see the road for my tears. I stopped and called our son Rob in Southern California. After I told him the news, he asked if I was all right.

"No." I burst into tears.

"Mom! You should not be driving up that treacherous road."

He was talking about Route 66 heading up Green Springs Mountain. On the best of days, people call the winding path to the sky treacherous. The narrow road winds with hairpin curves, steep drop-offs, and only a few guard rails.

I tried to lighten the mood by making a joke. "Well, that's one way to get this over with."

Rob continued to try to talk me out of driving.

I resisted. I had to get home to my husband. Cat needed me now more than ever. But when we ended our call, I just sat there. I rolled down the window and breathed in the rich scents of autumn. Still, the tears refused to stop. After several minutes, the phone rang. Without checking the display, I answered.

"Your son just called me," Steve, a pastor friend, said. "He thinks you're suicidal."

I assured him I had no plans to take my life at that moment. Then I explained everything to him. He surprised me by saying the diagnosis wasn't that bad.

"You've gone to the worst place first," Steve said. "You still have lots of good years together and even more moments."

Moments. Steve's words spoke hope to my soul.

Isn't that all any of us really have? This moment?

My tears finally subsided for a time, and I drove up the treacherous mountain road. When I reached our home, Cat pulled me into his arms and held me a long time. Then, we climbed the stairs to the loft and laid in bed together, soaking in the warmth and love of each other.

We stayed there for hours until my tears were spent and hope finally blossomed.

Cat and Sandy.

**Eagle Point, Oregon
March 2020**

"I'm broken."

Those are the most difficult words to hear from my strong mountain man who has never feared anything.

More than two years have passed since Cat's diagnosis. A lot has happened. God has performed some amazing miracles, yet we still face daunting hurdles. One of the biggest miracles I have witnessed is how closely Cat is now connected to God. It seems the more his brain's white and gray matter refuses to do what he wants, the more his soul connects to the spiritual realm. Because of that, I listen up when he has something important to say.

Lately, he's been telling me, "This world is broken."

I'm sure we can all see the truth in those words. And now, with this COVID-19 affecting everyone in some way, we can clearly see how our systems also are broken.

Yes. Cat is right. We live in a broken world. And many of us humans are also broken.

I've asked myself why God would allow this COVID-19 to spread like it is. He could stop it, yet He doesn't. And He has warned us these kinds of things will happen as we approach the last days and near the time of His reappearing.

"This calls for patient endurance and faith on the part of the saints," He says twice in the book of Revelation.

I'm wondering if He is allowing our world to be shaken so we can begin to understand our brokenness. We believers have lost sight of what is real. We have relied on our own thinking and our own strength for far too long.

Hebrews talks about how the things that can be shaken will be shaken (both in Heaven and Earth), so the things that cannot be shaken will remain. (See Hebrews 12:26-27.)

Perhaps God is allowing us to see our brokenness so we will return to Him. He is the one thing that cannot be shaken. He is the foundation on which everything good is built.

Eagle Point, Oregon
April 2020
Reality Check

Today, I encountered a brutal reality check on this very thing. We recently had to leave our beloved mountain home, and I miss our friends and church. We can't even see our family, because we must protect Cat from COVID-19.

Perhaps that's what made me overreact to something Cat did today. I don't know. What I do know is that I blasted him with questions he could not answer. Then I blamed him for putting me into a place of anger.

As my anger grew, he looked at me and said, "I would never talk to you like that."

As soon as he said it, I knew it was true. God had placed those wise and calming words in my husband's mouth.

I remained quiet while the ticking clock counted off seconds. But then I said, "Of course, you wouldn't. You don't talk at all!"

I left the room, hurting and ashamed.

In truth, if Cat had talked to me like I had just talked to him, I would have been completely crushed in spirit. How had I reached that place? Had I crushed his spirit? That certainly wasn't something I wanted to do. Tears streamed down my face.

Cat soon joined me, holding his arms out. "H-how—" he started, "How can I . . . m-make this stop?"

Part of his medical struggle causes him to have trouble getting his words out, especially when experiencing stress.

It broke my heart to see how important it was to him to make things right even with great effort. I fell into his waiting arms. Instantly everything was made right again.

Yes. This world is broken, but so are each and every one of us.

If we refuse to recognize this fact, we become arrogant and self-righteous, blaming everyone else for the world's problems. On the other hand, if we recognize and acknowledge our brokenness and fall into the arms of our amazing Creator, we discover everything is made right instantly. Because our Creator is also our Redeemer. That is why I call Him Creator Redeemer.

"But nothing changed," you say.

You are right. The pandemic still rages through the land, but on the other hand, *everything* has changed. For suddenly, we find ourselves basking in the love of our Savior, and we see the world through a much different lens.

We see hurting people, just like ourselves, in need of hope.

It's easy to act out of brokenness.

Often, when someone hurts us, we want to lash back at the injustice, but it rarely accomplishes any good. In my more-than-forty-year walk with God, I've discovered that walking the Jesus Way is not intuitive. World think is intuitive, but world think has caused all the brokenness.

God think, on the other hand, is impossible to maintain without Holy Spirit power.

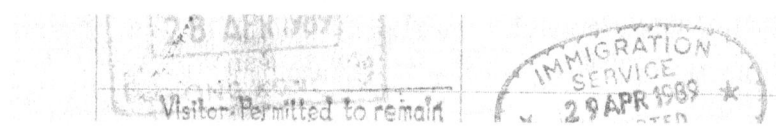

SECRET MISSION: LOVING BROKEN PEOPLE

1. In what ways or areas do you see yourself as broken? Take those before God and lay them at His feet. He is the great Restorer. When you realize how much your Creator Redeemer loves you, you will be more able to love others.

2. Are your words encouraging or hurtful to broken people? (You can ask God to reveal this to you and to show you how to change if needed.)

**Pinehurst School, Green Springs, Oregon
February 2020**

This is my second year volunteering as a "buddy reader" at Pinehurst School. I love that all the kindergartners I had last year are now in the first grade. We have an amazing rapport.

One day one of the boys was at home sick, which left Mack outnumbered by two girls. I had just given them a choice of books for me to read first.

Mack jumped up with his choice. "This one!" he said. "It's my favorite book in the whole world."

"Great," I said. "We'll start with this one."

The girls looked at each other. Then with a smug expression, one said, "Let's take a vote."

"Uh-oh," I said to Mack. "You know what this means?"

He stared back at me with complete innocence. He had no idea.

The girls did a high five, knowing full well they had won. I didn't need to ask them which book they wanted. The book had never mattered in the first place. It was all about the vote. They simply wanted to outvote Mack.

"You are outnumbered," I told Mack. "We'll have to do what the girls want."

His smile faded.

"Don't worry," I assured him. "I will read both books, but yours will have to be second."

I expected a fight, or perhaps a few tears, or at least a bit of rebellion, but Mack surprised me by being perfectly okay with the decision. After all, we had taken a vote. It might have been a different ending if we only had time for one of the books, but he was content that I also would read his book by the end of our storytime.

Voting is human think, and it comes in handy for many circumstances, but God doesn't give us a vote when it comes to His commands.

God says, "Love is patient, love is kind. It does not envy, it does not boast, it is not proud. It does not dishonor others, it is not self-seeking, it is not easily angered, it keeps no record of wrongs. Love does not delight in evil but rejoices with the truth. It always protects, always trusts, always hopes, always perseveres" (1 Corinthians 13:4-7).

This kind of love is God think.

Let's look at that more closely.

Love is patient.
Love is kind.
Love does not envy.
Love does not boast.
Love is not easily angered.
Love keeps no record of wrongs.
Love does not delight in evil.
Love rejoices with the truth.

> *Love* always *protects.*
> *Love* always *trusts.*
> *Love* always *hopes.*
> *Love* always *perseveres.*

When is the last time you saw love like this exhibited on social media?

Or how about in your own home?

I certainly wasn't giving out this kind of love when I allowed myself to become angry with Cat.

God's love never fails. But our love does. When we recognize we are not loving in the way God has shown us, we can stop and ask for forgiveness and ask God to love others through us. The above list is precisely how God loves us.

We can all be Secret Agents when it comes to loving broken people. We are all broken. We may not look like we possess the power to love others in this way, but our God has given us the ability to choose to turn to Him and let His love flow through us.

That kind of love always hopes and always perseveres. It never gives up.

Sandy in Kunming, China.

2
FRIEND OF GOD

> Greater love has no one than this:
> to lay down one's life for one's friends.
> you are my friends
> if you do what I command.
> —*John 15:13-14*

Green Springs, Oregon
March 9, 2020

A FRIEND CALLS ME her "Secret Agent Woman."

I always cringe a little, because I figure she means I don't look like much, yet God does amazing things through me. That should be enough, right?

But the pride and humanness in me want to look good. And that's the crux, isn't it? No matter how much we try to die to ourselves, there's a part of us that always sneaks up to grab attention. Look at me! Aren't I something? And as fast as it sneaks up, we feel ashamed, and then we sink to the depths, thinking we couldn't possibly be used by God at all.

In times like these, I put on a worship playlist, open my Bible, and remind myself of what is true and good and lovely.

> I am a friend of God.
> He loves me.
> Not because I'm an amazing Secret Agent Woman,
> but because He made me just the way I am.
> He has caused me to become His faithful daughter.
> He filled me with His Holy Spirit
> and He teaches me daily
> how to walk with Him.

So why is it, we so often feel like imposters? Can I really be a friend of God, the Creator of Heaven and Earth?

Chengdu, China
1989

I had told the girls Barry McGuire was a friend of mine.

"Yeah, right," said one.

"It's true," I said. "Don't you think Barry has any friends?"

Scenes from Chengdu, China.

They shook their heads and turned away. We were in Chengdu, China. A Chinese friend had introduced me to the girls. They were from New Zealand, and I learned they went to the same church as Barry McGuire.

Having been "written off" as a fraud, I stood nearby and listened as the three girls talked.

I was nearing the end of a month-long solo trip through China. I would have dearly loved to talk with these girls. I thought about the times I had talked with Barry and of how gracious and kind he had always been, as well as full of fun. I wondered if the girls were right. Perhaps I wasn't such a friend. After all, we were talking about Barry McGuire, the man I idolized back in my hippie days when he sang out, "Eve of Destruction."

I first met Barry through a church I was working for as a secretary, and one of my jobs was to book concerts. Instead of having me contact his agent, Barry gave me his personal number.

"I will always come to Southern Oregon," he said.

So, that's how Barry McGuire and I became friends.

Okay, we didn't call each other regularly or send cards and notes, but he always answered when I called, and he always treated me as a sister. That, to me, was good enough to be called a friend.

So why did I feel like such an imposter with these girls?

A Friend of God

What about you?

When you tell someone, "I am a friend of God," do they look at you and say, "Yeah, right?"

Does their reaction make you question whether you truly are a friend of God? Do you begin to feel like an imposter?

Or does it make you want to shout, "Hey! I really am a friend of God!" while they walk away, shaking their heads?

"Well, yeah," you might say, "I guess I'm not that close to God. I mean, I thought I was, but then when I think about it . . . ."

Jesus received the same treatment in His hometown when He told people He was the Son of God.

"Isn't this the carpenter?" some said. (See Mark 6:3.) "Isn't this Mary's son and the brother of James, Joses, Judas, and Simon?"

Because of their unbelief, He could do no miracles there, even though He was doing miracles everywhere else. "The blind receive sight, the lame walk, those who have leprosy are cleansed, the deaf hear, the dead are raised, and the good news is proclaimed to the poor" (Matthew 11:5).

If Jesus had trouble getting people to believe Him when He was performing such amazing miracles, then why should we expect anyone to believe us when we say we are a friend of God? Perhaps we should all become Secret Agents.

Instead of *telling* people we are friends of God, let's *show* them by our actions that the God of the Universe, The Maker of Heaven and Earth, reaches out to us in amazing ways and fills us with His Light.

Jesus doesn't say He'll *bring* us to The Light. Jesus *is* the Light.

Then He goes on to say, "Whoever follows me will never walk in darkness, but will have the light of life."

"I am the Light of the world," He says in John 8:12.

His Light shines in and through us.

"A new commandment I give you," Jesus says in John 13:34-35. "Love one another. As I have loved you, so you must love one another. By this everyone will know that you are my disciples, if you love one another."

That's how we shine the Light, by allowing God to love others through us. That's the love we love one another with.

That's why I didn't argue with the girls about Barry being my friend. That discussion would have served no good purpose, and it wouldn't have been loving. That same reasoning is why I get after myself for cringing when Jeanne calls me her "Secret Agent Woman."

I know Jeanne loves me and means well. I believe this because God has given us love for one another.

We should all become Secret Agents, not looking like much on the outside, but having a powerful love Light shining through us. This is an expected result of being a friend of God.

SECRET MISSION: BECOMING A FRIEND OF GOD

1. How do you know you are a friend of God?

2. Who can you share God's love with today?

Back in the sixties, we hippies loved Barry McGuire's song, "Eve of Destruction," because everything we had been taught to believe seemed to be falling apart.

Our young men were being drafted to fight a war that wasn't even called a war. Yet the Vietnam Conflict took as many lives as a war would. According to Britannica, in 1995, Vietnam released an official estimate of war dead. They said as many as two million civilians on both sides lost their lives! Add to that 1.1 million North Vietnamese and Viet Cong soldiers. Also, the U.S military has estimated that between 200,000 and 250,000 South Vietnamese soldiers died along with more than 58,000 American soldiers. Sounds like a war to me!

Justice was no longer prevailing, and we hippies wondered if it ever had. I wore hip-hugger bell-bottoms and walked through the park, passing out flowers in protest.

I wasn't against the men who were fighting. I was against the government that sent my friends to the other side of the world with so little hope. The Cultural Revolution was happening in China, and the United Kingdom was experiencing bloody riots and demonstrations. The entire world seemed to have gone crazy.

Barry's song spoke to our hearts. Better yet, he spoke what was *in* our hearts.

When Barry became a Christian, he again spoke what was in the hearts of a whole generation of Jesus Freaks. Like many of us, Barry was attracted to Christ but put off by what he saw as a hypocritical church.

Many of us (Barry included) discovered the war was not what was going on *around* us, but what was going on *inside* us.

"Everybody's trying to change the world," Barry said in an insightful article (April 2009) found at crossrhythms.com, "but the only way we can change the world is to change ourselves. To get, as Christ called them, the beams out of my own eyes."

Wouldn't it be great if we are on the eve of destruction of our own pride and hang-ups?

Now that's a destruction I can get behind. But that wasn't the kind of healthy destruction that was waiting for Cat and me back in 2017 or even now in 2020 when Barry's words seem more valid than ever. Certainly, we seem to be on the eve of destruction.

Will that destruction be the death of us? Or the life of us? As Secret Agents, we can breathe life and restoration into the destruction around us, because we know and believe we are friends of God.

Road of Bones (Kolyma Highway) by Magadan artist.

3
KINDNESS

> But to you who are listening I say:
> Love your enemies,
> do good to those who hate you, . . .
>
> —*Luke 6:27*

Pinehurst School, Green Springs, Oregon
February 2020

RECENTLY, THE FIRST GRADERS in my Pinehurst buddy reading were working on their writing. They were excited to show me how grown up they were.

"Gracie," I said, "your writing is amazing. It looks like a piece of art."

She beamed. Every letter was straight and perfectly placed.

"I wish I could write like that," I said. "I start okay, but as I continue, it keeps getting sloppier."

Gracie paused and looked at me. "Let me see."

I shook my head. "Okay, but don't say I didn't warn you." I grabbed a pencil and paper and started to write.

"Dear Gracie," I wrote. "I think you have the most beautiful handwriting in the world. When I grow up, I want to be just like you."

My first letters were nice and even, but by the third line my letters had become crooked and almost unreadable. I held it up for Gracie. "See what I mean?"

Her eyebrows scrunched together as she inspected my writing. Then she looked up and said, "I think your handwriting is beautiful."

"Really?"

I had to look again. Gracie had seemed so sincere I thought I must not have looked close enough. But the letters were exactly as I had first noted, each becoming sloppier and sloppier as I progressed. I looked back at Gracie.

She smiled and said, "I'm practicing kindness."

Ha! So she knew my handwriting was atrocious, but she had chosen to take the higher road of practicing kindness. Her choice made me rethink many of my choices in the days to come.

Magadan, Far East Russia
1991

I traveled with a Christian courier group to take free Bibles as gifts to Russia. We had been in Magadan, Far East Russia, for a week. We enjoyed the scenery, breathed in the salty sea air, visited museums and old gulags, purchased local handmade items, devoured fried meat pies, and fished on the Sea of Okhotsk. Each day, as we boarded the bus, I brought something new to the two young women who were our guides. Nothing big, just little treasures I had brought from home, including photo cards I had made and some little handcrafted angels. I sat in the back with the girls and asked them about their lives.

They seemed genuinely surprised I was interested.

Elana was of Chinese heritage, so I asked how her family had ended up so far from China.

"All political prisoners ended up here during Stalin's leadership," she said. "My grandfather was one of those people."

She told me a sad story about Kolyma Highway, the road we traveled. "Millions of prisoners worked on this road. Thousands ended up dead and were buried beneath it. Most of us call it the "Road of Bones."

She paused while I wrote notes, then she suddenly broke into my thoughts. "I don't understand."

I looked up. "Don't understand what?"

"You are so warm and friendly. All my life, I've been told Americans hate Russians."

I thought about my childhood and how I had grown up with fears of Khrushchev and the Cold War. Then I thought about how, at the start of this trip, I had been afraid Russians would not like me, because I'm an American.

"I heard the same thing," I told Elana. "I was told Russians hate Americans."

"Oh! That's the government." Elana waved a hand for emphasis. "The government is not the people."

Ask What You Can Do

I thought about Elana's words often during the next few weeks. I could see how her statement was true for Russia. They had lived through some terrible leaders—first Lenin and then Stalin—who had hurt their people in horrendous ways. But was her statement also true for America?

Had my government lied to me about Russians hating Americans? Was our government not speaking for our people?

I thought about my war protests. I had protested the government, not the men.

Suddenly, I realized my government had not been speaking for me or hardly anyone in my entire generation of baby boomers.

We had wanted to believe our government. We had wanted to believe we were making a difference for the world.

We were helping people, weren't we?

But then the My Lai Massacre had hit the news along with other Vietnam atrocities, and I realized for the first time that Americans could take part in evil acts just as much as anyone else in the world. The problem wasn't about whether I was American or Russian. The problem was about me being human and in need of transformation.

John F. Kennedy shook my hand back in the sixties when he ran for president. I will never forget his statement, "Ask not what your country can do for you. Ask what you can do for your country."

As I sat on that bus in Magadan, I decided the best thing I could do for my country and myself was to follow Jesus' example and love all people as if they were my brothers and sisters.

Jesus tells us in Luke 6:32-36, "If you love those who love you, what credit is that to you? Even sinners love those who love them. And if you do good to those who are good to you, what credit is that to you? Even sinners do that. And if you lend to those from whom you expect repayment, what credit is that to you? Even sinners lend to sinners, expecting to be repaid in full. But love your enemies, do good to them, and lend to them without expecting to get anything back. Then your reward will be great, and you will be children of the Most High, because he is kind to the ungrateful and wicked. Be merciful, just as your Father is merciful."

SECRET MISSION: PRACTICING KINDNESS

1. In what ways can you practice kindness in your daily life?

2. Where has God shown you grace and mercy? In what ways can you show that grace and mercy to someone else?

In the last century, most people I knew showed kindness in person. Acts of kindness were something we did face-to-face. Today, social media gives us opportunities to show kindness in an entirely different way, yet often we use it to do the opposite.

We talk about this group or that group of people, separating ourselves as wiser and better. Instead of unifying, we separate. We even go so far as to bring Jesus into our politics, leaving behind a road built on the bones of the hearts of people we have trampled.

Jesus never did that.

Never.

He walked Earth at a time of great political unrest, yet He never took sides.

Jesus showed mercy even to people who took his life, saying from the cross, ". . . Father, forgive them, for they do not know what they are doing . . ." (Luke 23:34).

It's something to consider.

Why do we often write things we would never speak, especially on social media?

Is it because we can't see the person on the receiving end? Then when they respond in anger, do we respond in kind?

Have you ever experienced road rage, getting yourself worked up over something stupid another driver did? Then as you move closer, you discover the driver is someone you love and respect?

So, it wasn't a stupid person after all. The person simply made a mistake, as we all do.

Everyone needs forgiveness. Everyone needs kindness.

I once heard a Christian singer share his testimony. As he sat in the sunshine on his porch, he leaned forward and looked straight into the camera. "I never again want to take offense."

His words burned their way into my soul.

Offense. Could that be what makes us unkind to one another? Have we taken offense at something someone else has done or said? That thought has made me look at my reactions in an entirely different way.

"Let me see others as You do," I pray, because my Creator Redeemer knows their heart while all I can see is the action. "And help me not to take offense."

We really can trust the Holy Spirit to work in us if we ask for His help in making the right choice. We also can trust that He will give us His strength to carry it off.

Unfortunately, I'm not always in the mood to practice kindness, yet, that unwillingness hurts me and others when I don't. Wouldn't it be great if we all become Secret Agents, practicing kindness and bringing peace and grace into an area where they are seldom shown, speaking words of life, and being warm and friendly instead of exhibiting the expected anger?

Now that's a choice I can get behind.

Toilet Paper Crisis.

4
BLESSING

And do not forget to do good
and to share with others,
for with such sacrifices God is pleased.
—*Hebrews 13:16*

Eagle Point, Oregon
March 13, 2020
COVID-19 Fears

I HAVEN'T BEEN FEELING THAT GREAT the past few days, so I missed my regular shopping trip. Friday, I saw a girlfriend needed help, so I gathered my cleaning supplies and headed to her house. The first thing I saw when I entered was several packages of toilet paper and a big bag of rice stacked against the wall.

Noticing my gaze, she said, "Our daughter brought us supplies. Everyone is hoarding toilet paper, and she doesn't want us to go out because we're elderly. She laughed. "How did we get to be elderly, Sandy?"

I shook my head.

All I could think about was the meager three rolls of toilet paper back at my house. They weren't going to last long. How could I nicely ask for one package? But soon, we were on to other things, and the toilet paper was forgotten.

The thought plagued me again when we carried the large packages of toilet paper into the bathroom. We were trying to figure out where to put them since my friend had no shelves. I thought about mentioning they would fit nicely in my house. Instead, I suggested she cover them with a pretty blanket or piece of material.

We worked for a couple of hours while her husband read us all the latest news regarding COVID-19.

When we finished, she offered to give me all kinds of things, saying she wanted to thank me for my hard work.

I told her I didn't need anything, but I wondered, *Could I have one of those packages of toilet paper?* Yet I never asked because her daughter had purchased it. Still, if my friend had offered, I certainly would have accepted.

The offer never came.

That evening I told my son I had to run to the store. "Don't bother," he said. "The shelves are empty."

"Empty? Are you sure?"

"Absolutely," he said, "and you probably won't even get in the door. Besides, old people should stay in."

Wow. This elderly thing was beginning to bug me. I didn't feel elderly (most of the time), and I could still think of myself as a young thing (if I avoided mirrors). Wasn't it just a couple of years ago I was wearing hip-hugger bell-bottoms and protesting the war?

So, I looked online only to discover no toilet paper was available for a month.

A month! Even that wasn't guaranteed. Those two-and-a-half rolls were beginning to look quite puny.

"You only get two squares," I hollered to Cat.

"We can use towels, and you can wash them," he said. "It's not that big a deal."

Yuck!

I decided to make it my mission in life to find at least one package of toilet paper. Surely, shelves would be restocked by the time the one package was gone. Again, I searched the Internet and called several stores.

No toilet paper.

That night, I had to blow my nose six times.

The following morning, I dressed and prepared to go find toilet paper. Surely, one store somewhere that had one package left. Just as I was getting ready to leave, a nurse friend texted to see how I was feeling.

"My ears and throat hurt, and I have a terrible headache," I said. "I was around a bunch of young girls last weekend and must have caught a cold."

"Don't go out!!" she wrote back with double exclamation marks. I knew she was worried about COVID-19. "You can't be around other people. Give me a couple of hours, and I'll see what I can do."

I appreciated her kind offer, but I didn't even have the cash to give her.

"I'll have to find an ATM," I wrote back.

Before she could answer, the friend I had helped the day before texted photos showing how beautiful her house now looked. She had continued cleaning after I left. Along with the photos of her home, she sent a Facebook post that said, "Until further notice: No one can stop by unannounced. We ain't sick. We just don't trust you around our toilet paper."

I wrote back, "I can understand about the toilet paper. We are down to three rolls and can't even buy it online."

I hoped she would take the hint and offer one of her packages.

Her only response was, "Oh no."

The lack of further texts told me I had placed her in a dilemma. She was torn between wanting to offer me some of her precious toilet paper or honoring her daughter's wishes and keeping it for herself.

On my end, I was torn between feeling bad about putting her in such a predicament and wondering what I would do if the situation were reversed. It caused me to ask myself, "What would Jesus do?"

I laughed. The first thing that came to mind was the loaves and fishes. When the multitudes were hungry, Jesus took a young man's lunch and broke the fish and bread into pieces. Then He prayed over those pieces and fed more than five thousand people with them. (See Matthew 14.) He even had leftovers.

Would Jesus take one roll of toilet paper and tear it into pieces so there would be enough for both my friend and me?

I realized I hadn't even prayed about my lack of toilet paper. Shouldn't prayer be the first place to start? I lifted my need to God and barely said, "Amen," when the phone rang.

Our daughter, Jocelyn, had found two packages of toilet paper at the store. She bought one for herself and was bringing one to us.

I learned several things from this toilet paper incident. First, I need always to take my needs to God *before* I take them to anyone else. He has ways of meeting our needs that are entirely different than anything we could imagine or think.

Second, I have no right to think badly of my friend for not offering part of her supplies. I might think I would have been generous if the situation were reversed, but there is no way of knowing for sure.

For instance, if she had given me some of hers, would I have returned it when my daughter brought me some? I hope I would, but I might have talked myself out of it since I only had one and my friend had several.

Third, we often think we are walking in Jesus' footsteps when we are actually walking far outside. Jesus touched sick and contagious people all the time. Mother Theresa followed in His footsteps by giving up most all her personal comforts to help others.

In truth, most of us fall far short.

Wilderness Trails, Oregon
1996
Winter Camp

Back in the nineties, I volunteered as a counselor for at-risk kids. In the summer, we slept in teepees under a star-filled sky, but in the winter, we all piled into a one-room cabin. My job was to keep the fire going all night while the girls spread out in sleeping bags from one side of the cabin to the other.

I'll never forget the time one of the girls ended up having head lice. She had them so bad that we could see them crawling through her hair.

Julie, the camp director, spent the entire first night washing and combing all of the girls' hair. Each of us counselors helped pick nits.

Until that time, I had thought I would be like Jesus. I wouldn't be afraid to help the sick, because I would trust God to protect me. But on this night, I discovered something very different about myself.

I had always returned the many hugs the girls gave me with a bear hug of my own. Some of these girls never receive hugs at home.

But on this night, I found myself crossing my arms and keeping a distance. When I did hug a girl, I kept a lot of space between us. And we weren't even facing anything life-threatening! It would have been a huge inconvenience if one of the girls had transferred lice to me, but I wouldn't have died from the experience.

I realized that night how far short I came to walking in the footsteps of Jesus.

Eagle Point, Oregon
August 2020

Recently, I received another opportunity to walk in the footsteps of Jesus. This time I chose the higher road.

Dale, my brother-in-law, was preparing for a visit to our new home. "Is there anything I can bring?"

"Just yourself," I texted back, then on second thought, I wrote, "and a Crenshaw melon."

"Unfortunately," he said, "they are no longer in season, but I will look."

Rats! I sent him a meme showing my frustration.

To my surprise, Dale arrived with my coveted Crenshaw melon. I immediately placed it in the refrigerator so it would be nice and cold.

That night our family came to dinner for the first time in our new home. The occasion demanded a celebration. It was painful, but I dragged out the Crenshaw and shared it with everyone, even though I was tempted to keep it for myself.

I'm so glad I didn't.

Several family members had never even heard of a Crenshaw melon, let alone tasted it. And wasn't it just like my Creator Redeemer to stretch that melon, so everyone who wanted some ate plenty? I even savored the last bite.

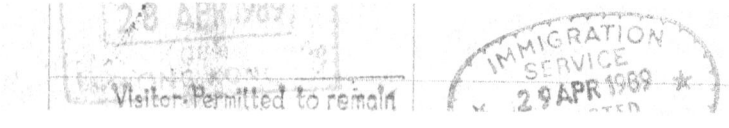

SECRET MISSION: WALKING THE BLESSING WAY

1. What do you own that could bless someone else?

2. The next time you see someone in need, ask God to show you if you can do anything for them, then do it.

**Eagle Point, Oregon
August 2020**

Cat and I recently moved. So recent that a lot of stuff remains in boxes. We have stuff in a storage shed; we have stuff in a horse trailer; we have stuff in two utility trailers, and now we have stuff in a double car garage.

We own a lot of stuff!

While we were packing, I kept saying, "Maybe we should give this away."

"Not yet," Cat would always say. "We might need it."

We gave a few things away, but not near as much as we should have. Then, one day, we were talking with Steve Evans, our wilderness outfitter boss.

"We have too much stuff," I said.

"I was the same way," Steve said. "I had this rifle I never used. I liked to bring it out and show the guys. We would all ooh and ahh over it. Then one day, I decided to sell it."

Steve went on to tell the story of how the young man who had bought his rifle was thoroughly delighted with it. The young man only owned one rifle, and he used it for all of his shooting needs. He kept calling Steve and telling him about the awesome things he was doing with that rifle. "Thanks for selling it to me," he kept saying.

The young man knew how difficult it was for Steve to let go of that rifle.

"It's been such a blessing seeing this guy have so much fun," Steve told me. "Now I look at my other stuff and ask myself, 'Who can I bless with it?'"

For some of us, that gifting is a tough choice to make. I tend to hang on tightly to my treasures. Unfortunately, I'm discovering that tendency is part of the brokenness in our world.

Because of Steve's story, I now have several boxes of stuff set aside to "bless" someone else. I've had fun asking myself, "Who would appreciate this as much as I do?"

If you have too much stuff, you might want to give this a try. Give away some nice things you probably don't have time for anymore. Don't just think of the people you know and love. Be open to whoever the Lord places on your heart. And don't give away only the broken and discarded things.

As Secret Agents, we seek God's help in making the difficult choice to bless someone else with our treasures.

Scenes in Kunming China.

5
LISTENING

> At this my heart pounds
> and leaps from its place.
> Listen! Listen to the roar of his voice,
> to the rumbling that comes from his mouth.
>
> —*Job 37:1-2*

Flying over Seattle, Washington
1989

I SAT ON THE PLANE watching the landing gear go down, and then go up, and then go down, and then go up repeatedly. I felt like Jonah on the boat.

"Throw me overboard," he had told the crew, "and the storm will stop."

"God," I whispered, "You don't have to put all these people in danger to stop me. Please."

The landing gear continued to do their dance as we circled in the air for more than two hours. Finally, the captain's voice came through the speakers. "Sorry to tell you this, folks, but we seem to be having a problem with our landing gear. We have been circling to get rid of our fuel, and emergency personal are waiting below. We ask you to keep your seatbelts buckled, lean forward, and place the pillows we've given you in front of your faces."

The stewardess showed us the position we should all take.

I continued to stare out the window. Lights blinked below. They must be coming from the emergency vehicles the captain had told us about.

"Please God," I prayed again. "I'll turn around and go home if that's what you want. Just don't let all these people die because of me."

"It's time," the captain said. "Use your pillows."

I leaned forward and sank my forehead into the small cushion, thinking about what had placed me into this position in the first place.

**Southern Oregon
A Few Weeks Ago**

It had all started when our original group of thirteen people had whittled down to two, one other guy and me. I knew it wouldn't be right for the two of us to go together, so I decided to send another man in my place. The two men could travel together. While Cat worked the graveyard shift, I spent the entire night reading through the Bible and seeking God for direction. I wanted to know if He agreed with my decision.

Finally, I believed I heard God say, "You can send someone else in your place, and I'll bless them, but I called *you*."

Through those words, I believed God wanted me to go, that I was the best offering I could give Him. But how could I travel through China for a month by myself?

I knew our assistant pastor was an early riser. As soon as the clock struck five a.m., I called and told him about my plan to send someone else in my place.

"I don't understand," Abner said. "You are the one who had the calling. Why don't you go by yourself?"

His words struck fear in my heart.

"Alone!" I gasped. "How can I travel through China for a month by myself?"

I didn't hear anything Abner said after that. Thoughts of traveling to China consumed my mind. How could a lone woman do such a thing?

Part of me was excited. *Yeah. With God's help I can do this.* It seemed the right thing to do after God told me I was the best gift I could offer. But the greater part of me was terrified.

After disconnecting the phone, I quickly dressed for work and sped out the door. As I pulled onto the street, I turned on the radio.

"So," the voice of Cal Thomas rang out, "you're asking what difference one lone woman can make?"

"What?" I said aloud as I flipped off the radio. "Is this for real, Lord? Are you truly asking me to go alone?"

For the next few minutes, I talked with God as I drove down the road. Finally, I felt His assurance that He was asking me to do that very thing.

I turned the radio back on. The first words I heard were from a verse set to music, "He who began a good work in you will be faithful to complete it." (See Philippians 1:6.)

I had to pull to the side of the road. God was in the car with me, as He always was, but I was very aware of His presence at that moment. I basked in the feeling of rightness until all fear left me.

During the next few weeks, God continued to give me many signs. He wanted me to make that solo trip.

Then on the week before my departure, I received a call from the Missions Pastor. "I'm sorry, Sandy," David said. "The elders had a meeting and unanimously agreed they could not support a woman going alone to China. We won't be bringing you up for prayer in front of the church."

My hand went to my throat. These were men of God! Would I die if I went to China after their proclamation?

The next words out of my mouth surprised even me. "I'm sorry, David. But I have to go. This is the clearest calling I have ever received from God." A blanket of peace settled over me as I continued. "And if I don't go, I will always question whether I am hearing His voice or not."

David didn't even pause. "I told them you would probably say something like that. These men are pastors. They don't understand the missionary call like you and I do."

Aah, sweet confirmation.

From that moment on, I prayed for God to stop me if He didn't want me to go. "You've shown me too many times," I told Him. "So, I'm going forward until you close the doors or stop me."

Still Flying over Seattle

Now, you understand why I was sweltering in that plane, with my head pushed against the pillow, thinking all those people were going to die with me because of my prayer.

But they didn't die, and neither did I. Instead, while I was still thinking, I felt the plane's wheels hit the ground. We bounced once into the air and then came back down again.

"Woohoo!" rang out through the cabin.

"Home safe," the captain said. "The computer must have been lying."

As we taxied, I realized a new problem. We had circled for so long that I now only had ten minutes to make my next flight. It seemed God might be cutting my trip short after all.

I plowed ahead of all the other passengers and ran through the crowded terminal. In those days, before tight security, travelers could go straight to their gates. Every computer in that enormous terminal was down. I ran toward the one desk where real live people could tell me where my gate was located. I couldn't even get near.

Hundreds of yelling travelers crowded around the two flustered people staffing the desk.

"Okay, God," I prayed as I ran. "If you want me to go to China, then you have to lead me to the right gate."

I ran to the first one I saw. No other travelers were in sight, but two stewardesses were filling out paperwork.

"My plane!" I yelled. "Do you know where it is?"

They looked up, startled. One of them asked, "Mrs. Cathcart?"

"Yes."

She talked into her radio, and the next thing I knew, I was shuttled out to the middle of the airfield in a minibus. Then the attendants wheeled a staircase over to the plane and opened the door. I climbed on board with people whispering that I must be an important person to receive such treatment.

I settled into my seat, knowing without one doubt God was with me. I was doing exactly what He wanted. And I did, indeed, feel like a very important person.

Later, I learned some kind of solar flare messed with computers throughout the world on that day. I've never seen anything like it before or since.

Did God cause that solar flare just for me?

Stranger things have happened.

Hearing from God

What about you? Can you look back on your life and see a miracle from God on your behalf? Was there a time you knew you clearly heard His voice?

Was it a long time ago? Or was it recently? I hope so.

I often tell people to go clear back to John 3:16 or that place where you first fell in love with Jesus and start all over again. What was it that made you fall in love with Jesus in the first place?

A friend of mine is an excellent example of this. Her name is Robyn. She writes amazing poetry, but Robyn also fights a constant battle with depression. Years ago, she brought me a huge pile of poems written on single sheets of paper, hoping I could set them to music.

I was excited about the prospect, because Robyn is an amazing person with a story that needs to be told. Yet the more I read through that pile of poems, the more depressed I became. Every one of those poems was written from a very dark place. They were written well enough that they took the reader to that dark place as well.

What was the use in that? Should we all sit around and get depressed together?

Then, about two-thirds of the way through that pile of sadness, I discovered a poem that made my heart sing! I set it to music. It is one of my favorites to this day. It offered the only redemption in the entire pile, but what a redemption.

I returned the poems and said, "Robyn, whatever you were doing when you wrote that poem, you were hearing from God. Go back to that place."

Oh, that we could all be Secret Agents in the way Robyn was! Even in her depression and sadness, she recognized that God may have given her something worthwhile to share with the world. The words of her song have touched many hearts even when her own was breaking.

Robyn's Song

On His wings I have soared
Under His wings I have found refuge
He has taken me from the valley below
High on a mountaintop

Listening

Drawing me closer
Drawing me closer to Him

He has shown me living waters
Great waterfalls
His love is ever flowing on me
Who am I to question Him
When His wonders I see
His love is ever flowing on me

SECRET MISSION: HEARING GOD'S VOICE

1. Describe your circumstances the last time you heard from God.

2. If you aren't sure, or cannot think of a time, then go before the Lord right now and ask Him to remind you of a time and place. It helps to sit still in quietness to hear the promptings He places in your heart and mind. Once you remember the place and time, sit still and remember what that moment was like. How can you recreate that moment? Sometimes this means going all the way back to John 3:16 or the moment you first believed. Be sure to seek confirmation from God's Word as well.

Eagle Point, Oregon
May 2020

This week I talked with my friend Debby and explained how I had started my online writing class in January 2019. We sat outside under an umbrella table, sipping lemonade and sharing cream cheese and crackers. The aroma of hydrangea blossoms filled the air.

"I was searching for my word from God," I said. "I always ask Him for a new one for the new year." I went on to explain how I had finally realized I might be getting old, and I had more projects I wanted to accomplish than I probably had time left on Earth.

"So, I took three months," I said, "and mapped everything out with sticky notes on foam boards. Then I asked God what He wanted me to start with."

"What did He say?" Debby wanted to know.

I laughed. "He said, 'I'm glad you asked, because I don't want you to do any of those things. I have something new for you.'"

Then I went on to explain how God had told me to teach an online class, as if I could hear Him talking in my head. After that, I sat down and mapped out an entire year's worth of studies. I was all excited until I heard God clearly say, "No, I want you to start right now and trust me each step of the way."

The result of that conversation with God was why Debby and I were talking in the first place. After a very successful year, God had placed Debby on my heart at the exact time He placed me on hers.

"How did you hear God?" Debby wanted to know. "How did you know it was Him?"

I sat back. Debby stole my heart when she was a teenager writing songs and singing them with an Irish voice as clear as my beloved mountain air.

"Oh, Debby," I said. "You know how. You've heard God speak. That's where all your songs come from. The way we hear God is by hearing Him speak in our hearts. When we see His confirmation in The Word (the Bible), we walk it out. The more we listen and act upon His voice, the clearer His voice becomes. The proof is in the results."

"Oh yeah. I know," Debby said. "But I needed the reminder."

We talked a bit about why we see God do these amazing miracles, yet when a new difficulty faces us, we question whether or not we are truly hearing God.

I pointed out that she had definitely heard God's voice when she got in touch with me. I no longer had her phone number, and God had placed her on my heart. The class I had just started was perfect for her. Not only that, I purposely left two spots open because I believed God had someone in mind I had not yet considered. All of it was God speaking and leading.

Today, we are both excited to see the result of His leading.

If I had not acted upon God's leading back in 1989 when I had heard His voice more clearly than ever, then I would not have trusted that still small voice that spoke to my heart in 2019 or all those many times between when He led so miraculously.

This is the way of faith, and it's an exciting way to live.

Our Creator Redeemer can use something as small as a gentle nudge in the right direction, a phone call from a friend at just the right moment, or something as universal and magnificent as a solar flare. He does amazing things through the most unlikely people and in the most unexpected ways.

Continuing to tune into God's voice, especially through reading His Word, is the beginning of becoming a Secret Agent.

Cat at Trapper Camp, Sky Lakes Wilderness.

Antelope Camp in Eastern Oregon.

6
THINK

> Do not conform to the pattern of this world,
> but be transformed by the renewing of your mind.
> Then you will be able to test and approve
> what God's will is—his good, pleasing and perfect will.
>
> —*Romans 12:2*

Eagle Point, Oregon
November 1979

MEMORIES CAN TAKE US BACK to a moment of time, and it feels just like we are there all over again. One such memory for me dates back to November 1979.

For the last seven years, we had been living in a home we had built with our own hands. No electricity. No running water. Nine months of the year, we had to walk a half-mile from parking our Toyota to reach the house. But it was our dream home. We loved it there in the wilderness of Southern Oregon, where our family of five grew to seven.

One fall day, I kept smelling smoke in the air. Very little rain had fallen from the sky for many months. A spot fire had started on the ridge across from us, so I thought that was the source of the acrid smell. I kept running outside to make sure it wasn't burning too close. Michelle, our middle child, was home sick from school, and I had just put her younger siblings, Clay and Jocelyn, down for a nap. All three were upstairs as I worked below cleaning the kitchen.

I had just finished wiping down my new counters when a scream split the silence. I dropped my cleaning cloth and ran upstairs.

Fire!

We had used particle board for the inside walls of our cabin. The glue acted like pitch. The entire wall was on fire.

I grabbed Jocelyn from her crib and handed her to Michelle. "Go!" I hollered. "Get away from the house!"

I grabbed one of my homemade quilts and threw it over the flames as I had seen in movies. Sure enough, the flames disappeared, seemingly smothered. But then, poof! The entire quilt burst into flames. I tried this technique two more times with two more quilts with the same reaction each time.

Instead of putting out the fire, I was adding fuel.

I turned to head back downstairs and nearly stumbled over my children. They were standing openmouthed watching me. "Out!" I pointed. "We all need to get out!"

After leading them to a safe distance, I told them not to come back into the house. Then I ran back inside. Cat had hooked up a big water tank to our house. Whenever it rained, the gutters drained into the tank. I turned on the tap, but no water came out. Thanksgiving was in four days. The pipes were frozen.

Realizing the house was going to burn, and I could do nothing about it, I ran to the living room, wondering what to grab. The first thing I saw was the piano my grandmother had given me. Could I push it through the wall? The scene seemed so surreal—no smoke downstairs and no sign of fire, though I could hear the crackling sound above and behind me.

"No, God!" I hollered. "Please!"

Smokey, our family cat, chose that moment to run in front of me. *Grab the cat.*

I chased Smokey down and pulled him into my arms. Then I grabbed my guitar and purse and headed outside. Now, I had a plan. I would gather the baby and photo albums and Cat's paintings. My brain was finally working. I dropped my cargo near my gaping children and turned to go back into the house.

What I saw forever etched my memory. Intense heat had melted the upstairs windows, and flames reached high into the sky. Leaves on nearby trees were already singed.

Instead of going back into the house, I grabbed my baby, and we all rushed to get as far away as we could. Our journey took some doing as we were all barefoot and traversed a shale rock road.

We lost our home that day—with everything in it. The kids took a long time to forgive me for not saving Tweety Bird or our puppies. For months I kept seeing myself going back in and grabbing stuff instead of standing there wondering what to do. Such thoughts would keep me awake at night. I would go before God, and He would remind me that I was grateful all my children were safe. That was the most important thing.

We had less than ten dollars in the bank and no insurance. We were homeless for five months.

I'm sure you can understand why that day lives on in my memory. I'm sure you have something similar that lives on in your memory as well. The impact of that day changed our lives. Before the fire, we focused on spending whatever extra money we had on something we could touch and feel. After the fire, we spent money on family vacations and outings.

What caused the change?

Seeing everything we had spent our hard-earned money on disappear overnight . . . Cat's paintings and sculptures, my handmade quilts and piano, our cast-iron woodstove and family heirlooms . . . all gone in a few hours. We learned the hard way that memories are really all we have.

These days we share wonderful stories of adventure and fun that cannot be taken away from us.

Or so I thought.

Eagle Point, Oregon
June 2020

Dementia is a cruel force. The condition doesn't just steal memories; it confuses them so that stories come out much different than how they had really happened. I find myself wanting to correct Cat on so many levels. Yet, whenever I do, it serves no good purpose. In truth, I have discovered we all confuse our memories to some extent.

Think back to your last family get-together. How many stories were told when someone interrupted, "That's not how it happened"? And often an argument breaks out, seldom to end well.

René Descartes said, "I think, therefore I am."

But what happens when we are no longer able to think? Do we then cease to exist? Who are we if we aren't our memories?

These questions plague me these days. We've all watched some loved one succumb to Alzheimer's or dementia until we can no longer see the person they used to be. Yet, at the same time, I've seen miracle moments that defy science. The more the gray and white matter of Cat's brain fails him, the more I see him tune in to God.

When he speaks a word of wisdom, I listen.

He spoke a word of wisdom when I began this book. I started with the first chapter that seemed to come out of nowhere. Then I wanted to stop and plan the rest of the book before continuing.

"Don't do that," Cat said. "Just write."

The fact his words came out with no stumbling let me know Cat was tuned in to God. He usually has a difficult time finding the right words and an even more difficult time getting them out.

"Just write the words as God gives them to you," Cat said.

I wanted to argue, but how do you argue with someone who is speaking the words of God? Such an argument can come to no good end. So here I am, writing as God prompts.

Cat came to the Lord the same time I did. We had just watched a Johnny Cash movie about his Jesus walk, and the pastor gave an altar call. While everyone's eyes were closed, I went left and Cat went right. We met up front, both surprised at the other. Then we joined hands and gave our lives to God.

Cat's change was immediate. Overnight, he went from an angry, in-your-face confronter to a kind, yet strong, leader. My girlfriend says he is the most changed person she has ever seen.

I, on the other hand, came slowly, bit by bit, a journey of ups and downs until I finally trusted.

As you can see in this book, I'm more open about my beliefs, sharing them with the world. Cat is more private, living his faith in quiet resolve. That's why I listen up when my Creator Redeemer gives him a word to share with me.

He thinks, but that's not why he exists. Cat exists because he is in God's mind. God's thoughts are what hold him, and all of us, including everything in the universe and beyond, together.

God thinks, therefore I am.

Medford, Oregon
1980s
Big Gulp Miracle

Remember those miracle moments that defy science that I mentioned earlier? Here is an example.

I first met Frank while visiting a nursing home. I traveled from room to room with my guitar strapped around my back and singing for whoever wanted to listen. Frank was the youngest person I had ever seen as a resident.

One day I was singing the following words:

> *I don't pretend to understand*
> *the things that God allows in man*
> *tears flowing freely from our eyes*
> *but this thing I understand*
> *He holds His children in His hands*
> *Each one who has called upon His name*

Even as I write these words, tears are flowing from my eyes. No. I don't understand. Why does God allow pain? How can He allow my husband to go through this horrible thing? He's the God of the universe. He could change it all!

Yet, He doesn't.

Then I remember the next phrase:

> *He knows our frame is but dust.*

> *He knows the deepest part of us*
> *And even in our weakness*
> *His strength is made perfect*
> *Peace that passes understanding*

I first wrote those words after hearing a friend of mine had committed suicide. Upon hearing the news, my legs gave out, and I fell straight to the floor. I'll never forget how my friends dropped to the floor beside me, offering support and comfort.

Annie couldn't be dead.

Yet, I knew she was. I also knew I had failed her. I hadn't been there when she needed a friend to see her through. What if I had prayed just one more prayer? What if I had made that recording of my songs she had asked for? What if I had obeyed the nudge of the Holy Spirit?

The accusations were strong and debilitating. Then God gave me the song—the above phrases followed by most of Psalm 139.

> *Lord, you have searched me and you know me*
> *You know when I sit and when I rise*
> *You perceive my thoughts from afar.*
> *You know my going out and my coming in . . .*

The song finally ends with:

> *Your love is so wonderful to me*

When I sang the song for the young man in the nursing home, his eyes narrowed to slits and his fingers clenched into tight

Think

fists. I knew he wanted to question me about the song, but he was unable to say a word.

I stared into his eyes and wondered what pain had brought him to this place. "I know you're wondering about the song," I said. "But God really does care. I know that even though I don't understand why He allows us to go through so much pain."

Later, I discovered Frank had tried to commit suicide by hanging himself after his girlfriend had left him. Instead of dying, he had been left in a vegetative state, unable to move more than his fingers or head. He could no longer talk. I also discovered he was fond of Big Gulps, a popular soda size back in those years.

So, every time I went to town, I bought a Big Gulp, took it to him, and talked with him. Sometimes I sang, but most of the time, I simply told him stories. I told him about our trip down the wild and scenic portion of the Rogue River. I shared how Cat had almost drowned and how that had seared my soul with terror. I had nearly lost the person I loved most in the world. I told him of happy antics with my children and my job as a worship leader for Applegate Christian Fellowship.

While I told my stories, I held the Big Gulp with a straw to Frank's mouth as he listened intently.

Our routine continued for months, me telling stories while Frank listened and never said a word. The nurses had informed me he was unable to talk. Then one day, I told him a story about how Cat and I met when I was a bartender.

"That was my BC days," I said. "Before I was a Christian."

Suddenly, Frank pushed himself up and said excitedly, "Tell me about it!"

"W-what?"

I thought I should call a nurse or something, but Frank's eyes were fixed hard on me with such desperation, I could not leave him.

"Tell me how you changed?" He was still holding himself up on his elbows, something I knew was utterly impossible, yet I was seeing it with my own eyes.

I blinked several times, and then I shared how Cat and I had come to the Lord, how God had changed our lives, and how God was faithful beyond what we could dream or imagine. I was still thinking I should get a nurse, but Frank's eyes were shining now.

A smile spread across his face. "Oh! I see! I see!" he said. "I finally understand."

With that statement, he fell back on the bed and never spoke again. Ever.

Years later, I met Frank's sister under other miraculous circumstances and shared how I absolutely knew her brother was with God. By then, Frank had left this world.

His sister grabbed me in a hug and clung to me for a very long time. "We wondered who had left the book," she finally said.

I had forgotten about that. I had left the book I had written, *Songs in the Night*, by Frank's bedside. Full of stories with a song at the end of each chapter, I used it to share the stories and songs whenever I visited him. His sister had now read the same stories and had come to the same conclusion as Frank. Our Creator Redeemer is loving and faithful beyond understanding.

Someday we will understand why He allows so much pain, but here in this world, we Secret Agents walk by faith.

We trust because the One we trust has proved Himself faithful, even in the worst of circumstances.

SECRET MISSION: THINKING LIKE GOD

1. Do you have a big question for God that you've been afraid to ask? Ask it now, in prayer. Then wait in stillness until you feel His presence. You may not receive an answer, but you can feel His peace if you take the time. If you don't feel His peace, then continue praying and go to His Word. Continue to do this as often as you need—daily if necessary—until you experience His peace.

2. In what areas of your life are you having trouble trusting God? Ask God to reveal the why behind your lack of faith. Is it because you don't see Him as wholly good? Or faithful? Are you unsure of His love for you? He says that if you confess with your mouth and believe in your heart

that He is Lord, then you are saved. (See Romans 10:9.) He also says nothing can ever separate us from the Love of God once we've placed our faith in Him. (See Romans 8:38-39.) Ask Him to help you fully grasp those facts.

My Native American friends often talk about how they can only tell their own stories.

"I can tell you my story," Warm Springs Tribal member Laura Grabner once told me. "I can also tell you how other people fit into my story. But their story is for them to tell."

I've always been impressed that Laura doesn't expect everyone's memories to be the same. I like that. A person's memories belong to them. If that's how they remember it, that is reality for them.

Because of this realization, I try not to correct Cat when I think he remembers something wrongly. I make one exception: if he remembers something in a bad way that was actually good at the time, then I will correct him, because I believe those kinds of false memories are from the very real enemy of our souls. Yet, for the most part, details really aren't all that important.

Cat and I have loved each other for nearly fifty years. I love him more today than I did yesterday. Neither of us is the same person we were when we married forty-nine years ago. Both of us have changed in myriad ways. He used to bring me roses. Now, I rarely see a gift, even on my birthday. I was thin. Now, I am not. Yet our love has stayed strong through those changes.

The challenge is not to compare each other with who we used to be.

An example of this is a friend of mine who was always trying to force her husband to change back to what he used to be.

"You're committing adultery," I finally told her. "You're having a love affair with a man who no longer exists."

At first, she was angry with me, but I encouraged her to list the current good about her husband and ask God to allow her to see him the way God does. This method always works if we are truly seeking God, because God sees the heart when we only see the outside. My friend fell in love with her husband all over again. The tragedy came in the fact her change was too late. He had taken too much abuse and walked out of a twenty-five-year marriage.

My challenge is to love Cat for the man he is now and not compare him with who he used to be.

When I focus on the current moment, things work better for both of us. When I look at what used to be and compare, we both fall into depression.

Scripture tells me to focus on what is good and lovely and true and just. That kind of focusing is a matter of choice. We Secret Agents can make the right choice to think like God, especially when we call upon Holy Spirit power. After all, Holy Spirit power is the glue that holds us all together.

God thinks, therefore I am.

Cows waiting to greet me.

Wonder Break at Antelope Sunday School.

7
WONDER

> Where were you when I laid the earth's foundation?
> Tell me, if you understand.
> Who marked off its dimensions?
> Surely you know!
> Who stretched a measuring line across it?
> On what were its footings set,
> or who laid it cornerstone—
> while the morning stars sang together
> and all the angels shouted for joy?
>
> —*Creator (Job 38:4-7)*

Eagle Point, Oregon
2020

ONE OF MY ALL-TIME FAVORITE LINES in literature was written by Donald Miller in the opening paragraph of his book, *Blue Like Jazz*. I can't tell you what the book was really about, but I'll never forget those opening lines because of the feeling of wonder they awakened in my soul. They read like this:

> *I once listened to an Indian on television say*
> *that God was in the wind and the water,*
> *and I wondered at how beautiful that was*
> *because it meant you could swim in Him*
> *or have Him brush your face in a breeze . . .*
> —Donald Miller

Today, I experienced that very thing. I'm writing now while still bathed in that wonder. But it came after a miserable day of receiving new old revelations. You probably know what I'm talking about. A new revelation, but not really, because the revelation was something I used to know.

How had I forgotten? Where had I slipped into the mundane? I was so sure it would never happen again.

The first new old revelation was in the physical realm. After less than five hours of sleep, I jumped out of bed to tackle my usual twelve-mile ride.

Once upon a time, I knew better. I had even learned the hard way back when I was young and invincible and could do anything. Back when I ran nine miles every other day and worked out in the gym, and rode my bike fifty miles at a time. Back when I skied and hiked and everything adventurous in the outdoors.

Rogue Valley, Oregon
1989

I was scheduled for a six-mile run the next day. I knew I should take the day off to rest my muscles, but six miles seemed like a piece of cake compared to the nine I was used to running. So, I ignored that piece of wisdom and tackled my early morning nine miles followed by a workout in the gym, followed by a few games of vigorous racquetball.

If that wasn't enough to kill all hopes of doing well the next day, I joined my friends for night skiing. All of us runners knew we should rest the day before a race.

But it is only six miles, I told myself.

The morning of the race, a friend asked if he could join me. "I know I can't keep up with you," Pat Nugent said, "but can we at least start together?"

"Sure, but when I want to sprint out, I'm going ahead."

"I understand," he said. "No problem."

The course was an easy out and back through level countryside. We started, and I was surprised how my legs felt like they belonged to somebody else. I couldn't find enough air. *Did I gain weight overnight?* My usual breathing techniques didn't work either. *Was there a strange humidity thing happening?*

Pat, running beside me, talked up a storm. "Wow, this is a perfect day, isn't it?"

I grunted something back, not wanting to talk because it would take too much air and energy. I'm sure Pat must have noticed, but he was kind enough not to say anything. Soon, people began passing us, people who had never passed me before. I started to wonder if I would even finish the race, let alone finish well.

Pat remained bright and cheerful beside me until he could take no more.

"Hey," he said, an apologetic tone in his voice. "Do you mind if I go on ahead? I'm feeling especially good today."

I tried to muster a smile as I waved him on. "See you at the finish."

I hoped I would see him at the finish. The turnaround still seemed very far away.

That race made me a believer in the words of wisdom I should have paid attention to much earlier.

Eagle Point, Oregon
2020

So, how did I forget all that wisdom and head out on my usual twelve-mile bike ride after only five hours of sleep? Not only that, I decided to make a feeble attempt to tackle Goliath.

Goliath is the biggest hill on my route. He appears just after the halfway point. On most days, I conquer him in second gear.

Wonder

Yesterday, I had to shift down into first and ran completely out of gears before reaching the top. To make things worse, my gears were groaning and slipping.

A truck drove up behind me just as I was crowning the hill. I was pedaling so slow that my bike was having difficulty staying upright. I feared I would fall over in front of that truck.

"Okay," I said aloud to God as the lone truck passed. "I know better than this. How did I get to the place of ignoring learned wisdom?"

I rode a little down the road then stopped to catch my breath. Snow-covered Mount McLoughlin towered in front of me. I turned to view the entire mountain ranges surrounding the Rogue Valley. It seemed I stood on top of the world here. Birdsong filled the air along with the clean scent of recent rain. Sunlight spilled in droplets across the fields. I climbed back on my bike and continued as the cows and their calves watched curiously in the field beside me. A few of the youngsters kicked up their heels and ran.

Words from the book of Job came immediately into my mind. "I hunt the prey for the lioness . . . I count the months till the doe bears her fawn . . . Can you call down a flood of rain?" I love that last line because I always picture a laughing Jesus calling down a flood of water upon Himself.

Wow. God is in touch with all these calves and their moms. He's enjoying this view right along with me.

The thought made me stop again, something I rarely do on a morning ride. It was as if I was experiencing everything the way God was at that moment, a Creator very much in touch with His creation.

Then, boom! It hit me.

God *was* there, very much in touch with me, in the same way He was in touch with the doe and the lioness. He was enjoying me like He enjoyed calling down a flood of water upon Himself.

I held my breath at the wonder of it, knowing full well a part of me was understanding something in a way I had never understood before. A revelation I could grasp but not fully hold. It was an old revelation, yet new.

It wasn't that I had forgotten God was in touch with me. "God is in the details," I often say.

I thought I fully understood that connection. I talk with God throughout the day, and my thoughts go to Him in every situation. But, yesterday, I understood His connection with me in a way I had never understood before.

Immersed in Spirit

So, today, I started my ride after a good seven hours of sleep. I also oiled my bicycle chain. What a difference! No groaning from the bike—or me.

I enjoyed a delicious morning of intermittent clouds and waking fields. Energy ran through every muscle. As I crowned the first hill, I wondered where my rooster was. He always greeted me with a good morning crow, but yesterday his crow was absent, as was the song of the red-winged blackbird. I never saw even one killdeer. Usually, several of them run along the road beside me.

"Where's my rooster?" I said aloud.

Immediately, the rooster crowed.

I laughed. "Really?"

He crowed again.

Then a flock of turkeys gobbled their good morning. All the animals were already waiting for me, each in position to be close to the fence as I threw out my usual "Good morning!"

They were waiting for a greeting from me just like they waited for a touch from their Creator.

I flew down the road effortlessly, knowing Jesus was right there flying down the road with me. I tackled Goliath in second gear, not even needing to stop for a rest. Then I saw my first human, an older woman sitting on her porch. She had probably watched me from inside on other days and knew just when I should be passing. I felt her loneliness and need for connection, so I gave a cheerful wave and said a prayer for her as I rode by.

When I made my turnaround, I asked for blackbird song and received it. I believed at that moment I could ask for a flood of water to come down upon me, and it would.

"Where's my killdeer?" I said aloud.

When none appeared, I thought maybe I had pushed my limits until I heard a small voice in my mind say, *"Wait for it."*

I pedaled on, nearing the top side of Goliath, almost out of killdeer habitat.

Well, can't expect everything.

"Wait for it. Wait for it," I heard again.

Then a killdeer ran out into the road.

Laughing now, I flew over the top of Goliath and cut through my wind tunnel, completely immersed in Spirit. I was swimming in my Creator. His breath was touching me in the breeze.

When I returned home and walked through the door of my house, I felt my body displacing the air. I was still immersed in Spirit. God's breath was sustaining me.

I relearned a big lesson for a Secret Agent woman. To be a Secret Agent, we must always be aware of our Creator Redeemer.

SECRET MISSION: IMMERSING IN WONDER

1. When was the last time you absolutely knew you were in the presence of God? What were you doing?
2. Perhaps you need to change something in your life schedule to be able to experience God's wonder. Or do

you need to pray for more awareness in the moment? Ask God to help you set your thoughts on Him at all times.

I also learned another lesson that day. Though I had oiled my bicycle chain, my oiling did not make my bicycle run like new. Cat had sneaked into the garage the night before and oiled all my gears and chain, much better than my simple spraying technique.

I wonder how often God uses others in our lives without us realizing He has done so?

Somebody is praying for you right this very moment, and you are probably not even aware of it.

Lately, I've been feeling quite alone. I get mad at myself for feeling this way because Cat is here. We are together! And, for that, I am very grateful. But all decision-making is now mine, and I miss being able to run things by him for his opinion. In those fewer times when he can offer something, I become excited and then begin sharing like crazy and overwhelm him.

Few come to visit with COVID-19 demanding distancing and people leading busy lives. I find it easy to feel like I'm all alone. But the truth is friends who are thinking of me and praying for me, even though they might not call or visit. And the bigger truth is God is right here with His arms wrapped around me even when I'm not aware of His presence.

I've learned to put on worship music and go to the Sacred Writings (Bible). They are the best antidote when depression hits hard. I've also learned that sometimes we just need to go to bed. Sleep becomes a great healer when our thoughts are going crazy, and we can't control them. Many times, when Cat and I are stuck and unable to communicate with one another, we simply go to bed and lie in each other's arms. Often rest is the best defense.

Ashland, Oregon
October 2017

The evening after we learned Cat had brain problems, I was scheduled for a one-woman art show for Masterpiece Christian Fine Arts Foundation. The scheduling had happened months earlier, so Cat talked me into going even though I was still in shock at the terrible news we had received. The show was held in the lobby and hall of Pony Espresso Café and featured music, food, and art. An exceptionally large crowd turned up that night. The loud and boisterous night smelled of coffee and sweet pastries.

I was still having trouble processing Cat's diagnosis and felt entirely out of place in that happy crowd.

The doctor had said not to put anything off. Did that mean we had a month? A year? Several years? Every minute I was away from Cat seemed a theft of precious time. I was teary eyed and often choked up as I led people through the display of my colorful lions representing the heart of my Creator Redeemer.

When people asked about my red eyes, I simply said, "We received some really bad news about Cat's health."

A strange thing happened toward the middle of the show. Small groups of people hovered around me as I shared the story of each lion:

NOTE: To see color photos of these lions, go to: www.scatsandycathcart.com

Compassionate One
*Creator rises to show you compassion,
meeting you where you are.
In His presence, we have no fear.*

Lion of Judah
*Creator is the Lion of the Tribe of Judah,
not far off as some have thought.
He is always near for those who have eyes to see.*

Listening One
*Creator hears our every cry for mercy.
Yet He often remains silent
because He knows we aren't ready
for the rescue that is yet to come.*

Bears My Sorrows
*Creator feels every sorrow we feel.
He holds our tears in a bottle and records them in a book.
He promises that one day He will wipe away every tear.
Sorrow and pain will be no more.*

Love is on the Move
Creator is out to get you!
But not to eat you.
He longs to show you compassion.
Come as you are.

On and on, I went, explaining the story behind each lion. As I did so, *Thru the Fire* stood out above the others. This is Creator who is not far off, but very near. He is the One who stands with us when we go through the fires of life. We may be hard pressed on every side, but not crushed; perplexed, but not in despair; persecuted, but not abandoned; struck down, but not destroyed. (See 2 Corinthians 4:8-9.)

Thru the Fire spoke to me like never before.

After retelling the story several times, I began to feel God's presence. Yes. I was hard pressed, but I wasn't completely crushed. Yes. I was perplexed. Why did God allow such an awful thing happen to my husband? But I wasn't in despair. I still knew hope. I still trusted that God had a good goal in mind, even though I couldn't yet see that good thing.

Yes. I felt persecuted by all the doubts surrounding me, but I knew God had not abandoned me. Even though Cat might be struck down—and, perhaps, myself along with him—our souls could not be destroyed. We would forever be united together with our Savior.

I sold more prints of my lions that night than ever before or since. God was using the lions to speak to all of our hearts.

An interesting thing kept occurring. I would take each group down one side of the hall and back up the other, but I kept forgetting one lion at the end of the hall.

"What about that lion?" people kept asking.

"That's *My Defender*," I said. "He's the One who fights our battles for us. He is fierce and powerful."

Invariably, people would remark, "He certainly is scary!"

Then it finally hit me. "You don't want to be standing in front of Him," I said. "This is what your enemy sees as Creator fights the battle for you. You need only stand quiet and still behind Him."

As we Secret Agents stand still behind our Creator Redeemer, we become spiritually aware. Once we have tasted this wonder of His power on our behalf, nothing else will satisfy.

Sandy and Judi in the Forbidden City.

Pastor Samuel Lamb sharing his Bible notes.

8
FAITH

Forget the former things;
do not dwell on the past.
See, I am doing a new thing!
Now it springs up; do you not perceive it . . . ?
—*Isaiah 43:18-19*

Letter from China
1988

"PLEASE, IF IT DOES NOT OFFEND YOU, it sounds like you have something real and exciting. Would you please introduce me to Jesus?"

These words were part of the letter I received back from a Chinese friend I will call Wang. It was the last of several letters we had exchanged during a six-month period. I had met Wang on the Great Wall of China when I had stepped into one of the parapets and discovered him and his students sharing a picnic lunch.

Secret Agent

I stopped and gaped at the food laid out before them, blackened eggs, bottles of a yellow-colored drink, and steamed dumplings. I didn't realize I was staring until Wang introduced himself in perfect English.

"I'm sorry," I said. "I was just wondering if those are the hundred-year-old eggs I read about?"

"Indeed, they are," he said. "Would you like to try one?"

I passed on the egg but accepted his offer of a small, wrapped candy. Instead of the expected sweetness, a burst of pure salt exploded in my mouth.

Wang laughed at my expression then explained he and his students were on an outing from Southern China—their first to visit the Great Wall.

"Mine too," I said as my two friends stepped into the parapet. After I introduced Julie Wheeler and Judi Zanitsch, Wang explained that his students were studying English and were delighted to have us join them in some fun. For the next hour, we played rock, paper, scissors, and shared songs from our respective countries. I ended up singing "500 Miles" by Peter, Paul, and Mary because the song is about being a long way from home. One of the Chinese girls shared a song that brought tears to our eyes even though we couldn't understand the words. Wang translated as best he could, but the song's imagery didn't cross over to English very well.

At the end of our picnic, Wang and I exchanged addresses. At first, I had to be very careful about what I shared or asked in a letter because he received his correspondence at his place of employment. The letters were read before they reached him. He could get in trouble if I talked about anything to do with Jesus or Christianity. There came a time when he was sent to Europe for six months as part of his credentials. While he was there, we could speak freely.

"Please tell me about the cultural revolution," I asked. "How did that change your life?"

He wrote back a sorrowful story of how the government had separated his family during the cultural revolution. His parents were both doctors, and they and their children were sent to different parts of the country to work as field laborers. This hardship felt especially difficult because their traditions valued heritage, and all of that was taken away. For generations, his family had remained in one place, and now they were scattered.

Wang worked from sunrise to sunset until his body was broken and his mind was starved for intellectual activity. He finally despaired of all life and called out to the sky for help. "But I received no answer."

I couldn't believe it. Out of more than a billion people in China, God had led me to one man who had done the same thing I had done more than ten thousand miles away in the Oregon outback.

I wrote back, "I, too, reached a place of desperation in my life, and I also called out to the sky, but I received an answer!"

I went on to tell him about Jesus, and that's why he asked me to introduce him. Unfortunately, Wang had already returned to China by the time I received his letter, so I would need to talk to him in person. Making another trip seemed an impossibility because of financial and family responsibilities. So, I began to pray for Wang, that someone would introduce him to Jesus.

Applegate Valley, Oregon
1988
China Vision

The vision came on a Sunday night while my pastor friend Rick Vestnys and I sang a song he had written about the life of Apostle Paul called "Come before Winter." While singing the chorus, I received a vision of Wang on a ferry with the wind blowing in his hair. It was so real I could smell the wetness of the wind. It was as if he sang the words of Rick's song to me:

> *Come before winter before the storms come.*
> *Come share my joy, my hope, my Son.*
> *Come and encourage your brother in chains.*
> *Come if you can before it rains.*

You must go, Sandy," the Lord spoke to me. "And you must be back before June first."

As I explained earlier, this was the clearest calling I had ever received from God. The only time I was given a specific date. If I didn't go, I would constantly question whether I was hearing from God or not.

Miracles became routine on my nearly month-long trip. Still, the greatest miracle of all was that Wang sacrificed his Communist Party membership and position to become a follower of Jesus.

I didn't know this until after returning home and receiving a letter in code. When I had left, he had promised to consider everything I had shared with him.

"It is a very difficult decision," he admitted. "Because I have much to lose."

The hard choice for him was choosing between the Communist Party and Jesus. Having both was impossible, but giving up Communism would affect his entire family.

I promised to pray for him. I left before June first, just as God told me.

A few days after my return to the U.S., Wang made his decision.

The entire time I visited China, students all across the country were leading demonstrations calling for democracy, free speech, and a free press in China. These demonstrations waere no small feat since everything was done by word of mouth. I traveled from south to north and east to west. Everywhere I went, students were protesting. The rising tensions culminated in what is now known as the Tiananmen Square Massacre on June 4, 1989. Reporters and Western diplomats there that day estimated that hundreds to thousands of protesters were killed in the Square. As many as ten thousand were arrested.

A university teacher, Wang's heart was with his students. He could no longer support a Communist Party that killed unarmed protestors. He chose Jesus instead.

A Stronger Faith

I've often wondered what would have happened if I had not obeyed God's call. I suspect God would have used someone else to reach Wang.

What a privilege and honor that God allowed me to be the one. I marvel that our stories were so similar, both of us calling out to the sky. And the timing was perfect. I introduced Jesus. Then God showed Wang the dark reality of the communist system.

As a result of seeing God work in such an amazing way, my faith became stronger so that I am more able to step out in faith on a daily basis. A 1992 article from a Northern California newspaper following that trip sums it up well:

> **Bible courier faces danger for the Lord**
>
> Says forget past, seek to please God
>
> ■ The recipients are grateful to get Bibles; many have been imprisoned for their faith. Sandy Cathcart urges believers to seek a closer walk with Christ.
>
> BURNEY — Does anyone care about people in persecuted countries hearing the Good News of God's love for them?

Faith

BURNEY—Does anyone care about people in persecuted countries hearing the Good News of God's love for them?

Sandy Cathcart sure does.

The Bible smuggler will be featured at the 10 a.m. Sunday service at Burney Christian Fellowship . . . The former hippie from the small community of Prospect, Oregon, will tell about the dangers and satisfaction of taking Bibles into countries that prohibit people from publicly professing their faith and from reading the Bible.

Mrs. Cathcart, 47, has traveled to China to smuggle Bibles there and to encourage believers in the underground churches. She's also traveled with a group of Christians to deliver Bibles to Siberia in Russia. Worship is now permitted in the formerly communist country.

"It's a wonderful thing to make the trips," she commented this week. "They keep telling us how it means so much that they are not forgotten by other Christians." Mrs. Cathcart said many believers in China and those countries are imprisoned and persecuted for their faith in God. She also is planning to make another Bible-smuggling trip. The trips cost about $3,500, and couriers raise their own funds.

Mrs. Cathcart said it's important to have a devotional time daily. She spends time each morning, praying, reading the Word and singing praises to the Lord. The mother of five said such times alone with God and Bible study are

> essential for having a vibrant faith. She urged believers to draw closer to Christ.
>
> She also enjoys finding God in unexpected places such as in the routine tasks at her home and in the beauty of a sunset. Mrs. Cathcart, who is a songwriter, poet and musician, came to Christ in her youth, then rededicated her life to Him in 1974. One of her favorite Scriptures is Philippians 3:13-14. It says: ". . . Forgetting what is behind and straining toward what is ahead, I press on toward the goal to win the prize for which God has called me heavenward in Christ."

I was out front about my faith in God because the reporter had surprised me. The entire time I talked on the phone with him, I believed I was talking to someone from the church in Burney. I thought they were writing up something for their church newsletter. I had no idea the article was going into a major Sunday newspaper read by nearly all northern Californians.

In Retrospect

I see a lot of interesting things in reading this old article. First, the verse from Philippians was one I had memorized when I was young, back before I had turned away from God for ten long years.

Second, that verse popped into my mind in its completion the day I returned to God.

Third, it still seems remarkable that I truly did make room for quiet time with God even while raising five children.

Fourth, it is important that we care about our brothers and sisters throughout the whole world who are going through the same kinds of sufferings we are.

The faith revealed to the reporter of this article would not have been as strong if I had refused to believe God and play it safe. Obedience came with great sacrifice but was rewarded even more. I was no one special, a hippie grandmother from a remote section of Southern Oregon. Yet, God had done great things through me and continues to do so. Heart speaks to heart, and a heart sold out to God speaks loudest of all.

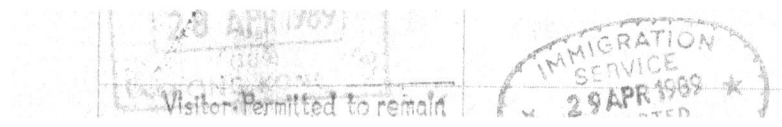

SECRET MISSION: STEPPING OUT IN FAITH

1. When was the last time you took a step of faith and saw God do something amazing?

2. Is God asking you to step out in faith? Are you afraid to step out? Ask God to give you confirmation if that thing is truly from Him or not. If it is from Him, then ask Him for the courage and faith to take action one step at a time.

Secret Agent

You may have noticed that I didn't use the term "leap of faith." That term is never found in the Bible. The expression is attributed to the famous philosopher Søren Kierkegaard. He argued that truth cannot be found by observation alone but must be understood in the mind and heart apart from empirical evidence. Since we cannot observe God with our eyes, he reasoned, we must jump from material concepts to the immaterial.

Many terms used in Christianity don't come from the Sacred Writings (Bible), and I believe they often harm our faith more than help it. The term "leap of faith" has many people thinking they just need to take a blind leap, leaving reason entirely behind, and God will catch them. Yet, the Bible says faith has real evidence and substance, and although we cannot see it with our eyes, we can see the results. So, we walk by faith, not by sight (2 Corinthians 5:7)—not a blind leap, but taking one step at a time, even though sometimes it "feels" like a leap.

Patrick Lundquist's *Leap of Faith* hangs on my wall. The painting shows a mountain goat midair leaping from one snowy pinnacle to another. The position of his feet look as if he will miss his destination, but his eyes reflect absolute assurance of a safe landing. He took the leap because he had full confidence.

Years ago, I stood beneath the statue *David* that Michelangelo carved out of stone. I went round and round, staring up at *David's* face in awe. Although the statue stands high above observers, we can clearly see that *David* possesses absolute assurance the giant will fall. That's the kind of faith that will bring visions to life.

I like the way gotquestions.org describes it. "A leap of faith is not an irrational impulse that causes us to jump out into the great unknown without any foresight . . . The stories in the Bible exist for a reason. Our trust and faith grow stronger as we read these accounts of God's powerful deliverance and rescue in times of need. God miraculously delivered Joseph from slavery and placed him in charge of Egypt. God transformed Gideon from a coward to a courageous warrior. These Bible characters took leaps of faith because they trusted in the God who was powerful enough to rescue them, hold them up, and not let them fall."

Jesus' disciples didn't leap into faith; they walked into faith one step at a time. Jesus lived His life in front of them in such a way that they ended up with the complete assurance that He truly was God in the flesh. Every one of them was willing to give their lives unto death for what they believed.

They didn't come to that conclusion overnight.

These are the reasons I like to talk about a "step of faith." But this is no ordinary step.

Do you recall the scene in *Indiana Jones—The Last Crusade* where he must cross a fathomless void? He has to take a "step of faith" into that void, believing a bridge will appear, which it does! Jones had been given wise counsel that a way would appear if he would just take that first step. He acted on that assurance with more than a little bit of fear, yet the greater part of him believed.

My point is that we really don't have to take a leap of faith and leave all reason behind. We do, however, need to examine the evidence and be willing to take that first step. Sometimes, that first step seems to be into thin air. Then as our feet find purchase, the next steps become easier as we see the wonder of God's leading.

In Tune

Remember when I told the Missions Pastor, "If I don't go, I will always question whether I am hearing His voice or not."

That's what happens when we *don't* take a step of faith after being given enough evidence to do so. And, the more often we don't take those steps, the more unlikely we ever will.

Secret Agents tune into the Word of God and His thoughts in our minds. Then we can take that first step of faith, trusting Him for each future step.

Helicopter dream ride.

9
BREATHE

> Then the Lord God formed a man
> from the dust of the ground
> and breathed into his nostrils the breath of life,
> and the man became a living being.
> —*Genesis 2:7*

Somewhere in Utah
2018

The first time Cat had a seizure, I thought he had died.

We were staying in a motel somewhere in Utah, the only night I didn't have reservations for our two-week trip. In the middle of nowhere with no obvious town nearby, we had stopped when we had tired. Our family was hundreds of miles away back in Oregon.

We were lying in bed, and I rested my head on Cat's shoulder as we usually do. Cat's head was propped up on a pillow, and my laptop sat on another pillow on my tummy where both of us could watch a movie. I have no idea what movie we were watching. That information has fled my memory, but I'm sure it wasn't as exciting or life-threatening as what played out in our room.

I simply heard Cat say, "Oh no."

Not loud like a cry for help, it sounded more like he had forgotten something. Lying as I was on his chest, I couldn't see his face, so I waited for his explanation. It's not unusual for him to remain quiet, so I finally asked, "What's the matter?"

No answer.

But that wasn't unusual either. Cat often takes time before he answers. One of his favorite sayings is, "Better to keep your mouth shut and be thought a fool than to open it and prove it to be so."

Finally, when no answer came, I turned and discovered his eyes and mouth wide open. "Dear God!" I screamed.

I pushed the laptop to the foot of the bed and began feeling for a pulse. None. His chest remained still. He wasn't breathing.

"God!" I screamed again. "Please! Don't take Cat."

I couldn't find a good position to do mouth-to-mouth resuscitation. I jumped out of bed and tried to pull on my robe. I wanted to be covered when I called 9-1-1, but sliding my arms into the sleeves proved impossible. My body shook, and I was still screaming out to God.

"Please, God! Please!"

Several things flew through my mind at once. I thought to call 9-1-1, but I had no idea how far away emergency services were, and Cat needed to breathe. I also thought to call the motel clerk, but that would take too long.

One thought rose above all: *Cat needs to breathe.*

I threw my bathrobe to the floor and ran around the end of the bed, hoping to maneuver into a good position to resuscitate Cat. By the time I reached his side, he was breathing, but he was far from okay. About three minutes had passed. His eyes were focused, but he remained unable to move or speak.

In hindsight, that would have been a good time to call for help, but I was useless. I fell on Cat's chest and wept with relief.

After a bit, his right arm came around my back—the gesture was his way of comforting me. He still couldn't talk. Then, when he could, nothing but gibberish came out.

For the next half hour, I leaned against him and prayed. Slowly, Cat's cognition returned. When he could speak, I kept asking him questions to make sure there weren't any residual effects. I wanted to take him to a hospital to be checked, but he insisted I not call anyone.

I stayed awake the rest of the night, watching his chest rise and fall. I felt his heartbeat beneath my hand, and I begged God to let me keep my husband.

The following morning, we headed to Zion National Park, Cat's favorite place on Earth. I saw no change in his speech or personality or mobility, so I thanked God and soaked up every minute we had together. I suspected this would be our final long journey, and I wanted every memory seared into our minds.

On the last day of our vacation, I called our son Rob. "I'm thinking about forking out a thousand dollars for a helicopter trip," I said. "It's something we've always wanted to do, but we can't really afford it." I had already told Rob about the scary night when his dad had quit breathing for more than three minutes.

"Well, Mom," Rob said. "I think you might regret it if you don't."

He was right.

That helicopter trip is something neither of us will ever forget. At least, I hope Cat won't forget. With dementia, we never know. But for now, the ride is one of his favorite memories.

Our experience was so amazing, flying straight toward a mountain. Then the helicopter pulled up, jumped over the top, and sank into the Grand Canyon. We were flying below the Skywalk.

To top it off, the pilot flew us to a sun-drenched mesa. We breathed in the smell of sage while enjoying a picnic dinner. I leaned against Cat while we watched the sky turn red and purple until the stars began to twinkle. We flew back to Las Vegas soaked in color, the stars above and bright lights below.

I'm so glad we chose to make and cherish that memory before it was too late. It reminds us: do not miss the magic of the moment.

Moments count.

Terrifying Moments

But not all moments are good. The rest of that year and all of 2019 were filled with terrifying moments as Cat's seizures came more often.

I took him to the hospital to have him checked out, but the emergency room doctor tried to convince me that Cat had fainted. She kept talking about fainting goats while I looked at her incredulously. If she had known anything about my fearless, mountain man husband, she never would have suggested such a thing.

Later, one doctor, who had spent a lot of time with Cat beforehand, did a CT scan. He kept shaking his head while looking between the scan and Cat. "I can't rectify what I see on the scan and what I see in this man," Dr. Presti kept saying. "There should be no way he can function like he does with such severe white matter disease."

That news didn't surprise me either. My husband is a fighter, and this was the biggest battle of his life.

Dr. Presti put Cat on a BiPAP machine. From that moment on, I saw gradual improvement until the day everything went south.

**Jenny Creek, Green Springs, Oregon
July 8, 2019
A Terrible, Horrible, No Good Day**

Cat had slept in because he wasn't feeling well on this particular day. I checked on him several times. When he finally got up, he looked pale and wobbly, so I brought him coffee while he sat in his favorite chair.

Suddenly, his body went rigid, going into a full seizure. Cat had experienced several seizures by now, and he always tried to fight them.

I did my best to keep him from getting hurt. That's what the doctors had told me to do while I timed the seizure and waited it out. But this one was different.

His body had never gone that rigid before. His head was back as he began vomiting.

I pulled as hard as I could, but I couldn't bring his head forward.

This position was dangerous, and he was probably aspirating. Vomit sprayed everywhere.

I prayed through hiccupping sobs for God to please save my husband.

He was shaky and confused when he finally came to, but I couldn't keep him from heading to the shower.

"No," I insisted. "You're too wobbly. If you fall, I will never be able to get you up. We need to head to the hospital."

He completely ignored me, as if he hadn't heard a word.

Four times I called his best friend. Four times I hung up before Pastor Joe Johnson answered.

Finally, Joe called back.

With no explanation, I said, "We need you. Please come."

Between the two of us, Joe and I talked Cat into going to the hospital. By the time we arrived, Cat couldn't even stand. I placed him in a wheelchair and rushed him to the emergency room.

His entire body shook.

"Does he always shake like this?" one of the technicians asked.

"No. Not at all." I didn't offer any more information, because of the "fainting goat" incident with the former emergency room doctor. This time, my silence almost cost Cat his life. The technicians decided he wasn't in any immediate danger, so they sent us back to the waiting room.

"Please," I begged. "At least bring him a blanket to stop the shaking and shivers."

They promised to do so, but the blanket never came.

Soon, Cat wasn't making any sense. I leaned down and tried to keep him warm by pressing my body against his as much as possible. He was burning with fever when he went into another seizure.

I called to the two young women, sitting behind an open window, whose job it was to check in patients. "Help!" I cried. "Please. Help!"

To my horror, they closed the window and stood with their backs to me. I burst into tears, sobbing loudly. If we couldn't get help at a hospital, where could we get help?

Cat shook like crazy, burning up with fever. He didn't even know who I was.

Part of me understood hospital regulations. Cat had been checked out and didn't appear to be in immediate danger, so he would have to wait in line with all the other patients who had arrived before us.

All those patients were staring at us now. "Please," I begged through my sobs. "Somebody help."

One man stood up and yelled at the top of his lungs. "Get somebody out here! I saw somebody die just like this."

I was thankful for his help, but his pronouncement didn't do anything to calm my fear. By now, I was shaking nearly as badly as Cat.

An orderly walked out—walked!—then he took the wheelchair and calmly pushed Cat into a consult room. "Everything is fine," he said. "Your husband isn't in any danger."

"Fine?" I yelled. "He's burning up, and he doesn't even know who I am. He is not fine!"

A flicker of alarm flashed over the orderly's face when he touched Cat's forehead. He picked up his pace as he left to retrieve a thermometer. When he read 105, things sped up significantly.

Cat remained in the hospital for two weeks. Most of the time, he wasn't even aware of what was going on. He had indeed aspirated, which caused the infection to run through his entire body and into his blood.

I stayed with him, praying the entire time. I accept the miracle that my husband is alive today.

Changing Tactics

From that moment on, I became proactive in Cat's medical care, insisting we find out what was at the root cause. I lived with him. I knew he didn't have Alzheimer's as one doctor diagnosed and that he hadn't fainted as the emergency room doctor had said. No one gave us any hope until authorities finally granted my request to send Cat to Portland VA Medical Center. We finally received a precise diagnosis of Cerebral Amyloid Angiopathy and medicine to stop the seizures and slow the dementia.

That diagnosis became the first ray of hope in a long line of increasing darkness.

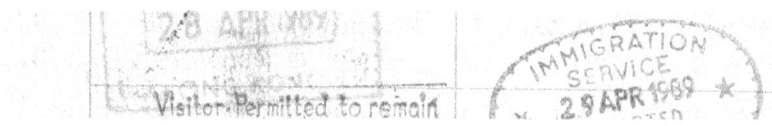

SECRET MISSION: BREATHING LIFE

1. What terrifies you? Take that thing in prayer before your awesome Creator Redeemer. Ask Him to help you know His truth that will set you free from that terror. I always find it helpful to remember how much God loves me and how much He loves the people I love. He loves them even more than I do!

2. How has God met you in your past hour of terror? Remembering how God has worked in past situations helps us have faith in His faithfulness in current and future situations.

Our Creator Redeemer is in the details. There is nothing too big and nothing too small that He does not know of it. He is not a big one of us. He is something totally *other*.

For several years, Cat and his siblings joined their father in Cabo San Lucas for a Christmas trip. While he went there, I watched movies on DVD, something Cat doesn't enjoy. The last time he was away, I watched two movies that made a tremendous difference in my life. The first, *Breathe,* was based on the true story of Robin Cavendish and produced by his son, Jonathan.

Robin and his wife, Diana—adventurous, fun-loving people— were constantly surrounded by friends. Living in Kenya, they had only been married for two years when Robin was diagnosed with polio. He was soon paralyzed from the neck down and was placed on a mechanical respirator. Twenty-four-year-old Diana was pregnant with their first child at the time. Robin wasn't expected to live more than a few months.

Because the movie is produced by his son, it candidly follows Robin's life. I was struck by the fact that one person can make such a tremendous difference.

One wife made a difference for her husband against both a system and a disease. The faithfulness of his wife impacted me. She never gave up on Robin and never remarried. Most people would have given up. Instead, Diana broke new ground, taking her severely depressed husband home after a year in the hospital, against the advice of his doctors. She pursued a plan that involved a loving home atmosphere that would lift Robin out of his depression.

One friend made a difference by persevering against all odds. Scientist Dr. Teddy Hall kept tinkering and designing until he came up with new inventions that would not only make Robin's life better but also would improve the lives of hundreds of thousands of people. He designed a wheelchair with a built-in respirator. The device, a model for future designs, gave Robin freedom from his bed. Hall relentlessly searched for inventions that would improve Robin's life.

One man made a difference for generations following after him. Robin campaigned for disabled people by traveling the world in his wheelchair and special van that Dr. Teddy Hall had designed for him. He raised money so others could enjoy a life of less restriction. Largely due to Robin, disabled people are no longer left hooked up to a machine. His list of accomplishments is truly amazing. He became a medical phenomenon as one of the longest-living polio survivors in Great Britain.

I took two main things from this story. First, we do not have to accept a doctor's diagnosis as the final say.

Doctors said we had no hope of Cat improving. When I believed that diagnosis it hurt both of us. We saw nothing but a bleak future where each day grew continually worse. Appearances seemed to agree with that diagnosis. Cat's seizures came more often and hit him harder. Confusion took over his brain to where he couldn't even state his birth date.

Frustration became the new normal. Everything the doctors had predicted was coming to pass.

Even while I watched the movie, I worried if Cat would have a seizure while with his family in Cabo. Would they know what to do? Would I?

The second thing I took from Robin's story was how one person can make a difference. Diana Cavendish has become my hero and the person I most want to emulate. Often, I fall far short, but I keep going back to God for renewed strength and energy. He never fails me.

The Greatest Showman, a spectacular performance of music and visionary explosions, was the other movie I watched. One scene will always stay in my mind of Zac Efron and Zendaya as they performed the most amazing acrobatic stunts to the song, "Rewrite the Stars."

Yes! Cat and I can rewrite the stars, because we serve the Maker of the stars.

Eagle Point
September 2020

Cat and I have walked further into our story now. I can say for certain things have not turned out as bleak as the doctors diagnosed. Cat is actually doing better in many ways. I never skip one day in praying for continued healing for him.

Secret Agents take time to breathe in the breath of God and know that the end is not the end until the end. And then, the end is truly just a new beginning. We have an eternity to walk with our Lord and with each other.

The beginning is near, simply a breath away.

Cottage yard on a spring morning.

Cottage in winter.

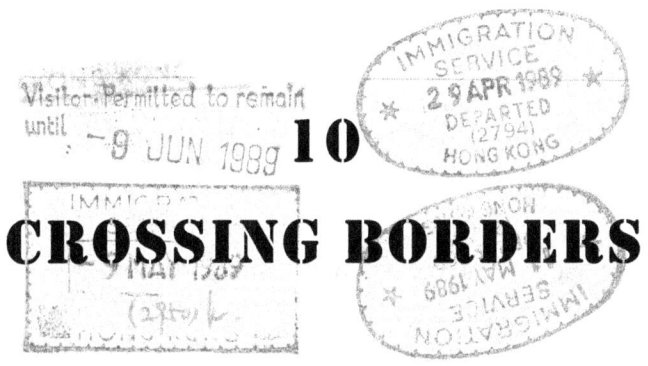

10
CROSSING BORDERS

> Very truly I tell you,
> whoever hears my word and believes him who sent me
> has eternal life
> and will not be judged
> but has crossed over from death to life.
>
> —*John 5:24*

Jenny Creek, Green Springs, Oregon
December 2019

WE HAD BEEN LIVING IN A GLASS HOUSE for nearly seven years, a snow globe in winter and a gateway to the wilderness. The small cottage with floor-to-ceiling windows was our perfect dream home overlooking a pond surrounded by a sun-drenched meadow.

Each morning fog drifted up from Jenny Creek and turned the sprawling park-like area to the side of our cottage into a magical wonderland. Sunlight would split into cascading ribbons as it poured through ancient tall timber. Not a morning dawned that I didn't wake up and thank God for such a gift.

The gift had been given to us at a time when depression hit me so hard that I could barely climb out of bed. My father had died three years before. My being an only child meant I took care of my ailing mother. In those years, it seemed that I spent more time at Momma's house than my own. Momma suffered from agoraphobia, finding it extremely difficult to leave her home for any reason, so I had to go to her.

When I first noticed her agoraphobia, back when Dad was alive, she hadn't been out of her house for years. Dad dragged her to family functions at our youngest son's house, but she never stayed long. I talked Momma into going out midmorning when traffic was light to a nearby grocery store and a library. That was her entire world. She much preferred the safety of her double-wide manufactured house and the beautiful yard and garden Dad had carved out of the field behind their mobile home park.

If Momma and I had been close, it would have been a joy taking care of her. I wanted to help grant her wish to stay in her own home and never transition to a full-time care facility.

But we weren't close.

She constantly reminded me of that fact. "I love you," she often said, "but I sure don't like you."

Hugs never went along with that statement, so the love part was completely lost on me. Fact is, I don't remember my mother hugging me. I'm sure she must have when I was very young, but the memory is completely lost.

Perhaps, that's why I was never a hugging person. People who know me now will laugh at that statement, but my husband and children were the only people I ever hugged until Esther Rhea came into our lives.

Central Point, Oregon
1977
A Persevering Hugger

Esther, our pastor's wife and a small bundle of joy and laughter, made it her goal in life to hug everyone who poured out of the service on Sunday morning. I knew it was coming and would usually hold a child in my arms to avoid her full-on hug.

That didn't stop Esther. She would hunt me down and catch me when my arms were empty.

I never hugged her back. Instead, I would stand stiff-armed, thinking she would catch the hint that I don't like hugs. Finally, I reached the point where I decided not to go through those sanctuary doors on my way out of service.

One Sunday, I snuck through the choir loft and departed through the baptistry and up the back hallway. I was sure Esther would be busy at those sanctuary doors greeting everyone else.

Instead, she met me in the middle of the hallway and gave me a full-on hug.

I stood there with my arms hanging limp at my sides.

"Oh, Sandy," she laughed. "I'm going to get you out of that."

For the first time, I realized Esther knew I didn't like hugs. All the times before, I thought she just didn't get the hint.

But she knew! And she was determined to change me.

I don't remember when it first happened, but Esther's persistence paid off. These days, I hug everyone and tell people I love them, because I don't believe we hear those words often enough.

But I never really got through to my mother.

Momma and Me

Momma hugged other members of our family, but whenever I tried to hug her, she gave me the same treatment I had given Esther. She would stiffen and let her arms hang limply at her sides.

I talk a lot about my relationship with my mother in my book, *Wild Woman: A Daughter's Search for a Father's Love*. It took my father's death for me to realize I needed to take the first step in doing something to heal our relationship. I always had been waiting for Momma to reach out to me. So, my first step was to be there for her in her final years.

I wasn't the person she wanted as a caregiver. She had hoped a favorite grandchild or great-grandchild would come to her rescue. Neither were able to leave their busy lives and faraway homes.

When Dad was in the hospital, there was a point that neither Momma nor I could think of one happy memory between us.

The first potential good memory that came to my mind was when my mother and I played a game of jacks on our hardwood floor. I was about nine years old at the time.

Though it should have been a good memory, it ended badly. My mother got an enormous splinter beneath her fingernail. Dad rushed her to the hospital while she cried out in pain.

She never played jacks with me again.

Jenny Creek, Green Springs
2012
The Perseverance of Esther

So, that's part of why I was depressed the first time I came to Mark and Jeanne Randall's ranch on Jenny Creek. Jeanne had asked us to stay in their home for three months while they traveled south to warmer weather.

As we drove up the driveway, I spotted a cottage at the far end of their backyard. Snow covered the forest, and the scent of fir and pine trees created the perfect scene for Christmas, which was only weeks away. I looked at the cottage's gleaming wall of windows and thought how wonderful it would be to create in such a place.

We entered the Randall's house and shrugged off our coats. "What is that cottage back there with all the windows?"

"That's our cottage," Mark said. "You can live there if you want."

I laughed.

Mark was on some heavy prescription drugs at the time because of some ongoing health problems. I could tell by the expression on Jeanne's face that he may have spoken too soon. Still, my heart leaped at the possibility of being able to live in such a place.

Our home in Prospect was no longer a sanctuary for me. Once located in the middle of the woods, during the seventeen years we lived there, the neighborhood became a subdivision—noisy and busy with no privacy. People either lived there because they loved the country or they wanted to get away from the law. Two meth labs operated across the gravel road from us.

The other reason I was depressed was that I had entered a contest with a piece of writing I was sure would win. After it made the top ten in the previous year, I had polished it to perfection. Or so I thought. This time, I didn't place at all.

I was sure I had written what God had wanted me to write. It even had a higher purpose for a group of Native American friends of mine. The rejection left me feeling I could no longer hear God's voice, and I doubted my skills as a writer.

So, we jumped at the chance to live in Mark and Jeanne's house while they traveled south. During their absence, I used the cottage as my art studio, enjoying many long hours of creativity with a fire crackling in the wood heater and the smell of peppermint tea wafting around me. That winter became a glorious time of healing.

When Mark and Jeanne returned, they invited us to stay in their cottage for a few months. We took them up on the offer. Nothing but peaceful forest surrounded the cottage. We watched deer, foxes, and bobcats meander in front of our porch. We stepped into cross-country skis and trekked from our backdoor up the mountain and back. We listened to worship music and felt the love of God healing our hearts. This was all before Cat's diagnosis. God was strengthening us for dark days ahead, though we didn't know it at the time.

We stayed until I received a call from my mother that she needed me. We packed our bags, and Cat returned to Prospect while I moved in with Momma.

During those last months of my mother's life, I made it my goal to create some good memories between us. I latched onto the persistence of Esther in her pursuit of getting me to receive her hugs, and it worked! I now cherish two good memories.

One happened when I stopped at a local specialty store and bought Momma two chocolate cupcakes. Her eyes lit up at the sight. She ate one immediately. Later, after dinner, she sat across the table from me and said, "I hear that cupcake calling my name."

I still hold that picture of Momma in my mind. She looked so beautiful and young, completely unguarded. Her voice was full of happiness and spunk. I think God revealed her heart to me at that moment—so different from what I usually saw on the surface.

My other memory is of the two of us watching the Gaithers on TV. Cat and I don't watch TV, and the Bill Gaither family performed music I didn't think I liked. But they grew on me. I have beautiful memories of my mother and me sitting together, in separate chairs, but enjoying the same thing.

That might not seem like a lot. And it's true that I have more bad memories than good. I spilled a lot of tears in those final years, all because of the hate I thought I saw coming from my mother toward me. I could do nothing right. But love is a choice, and I chose to focus on the good as my Creator Redeemer tells me to do. (See Philippians 4:8.)

So now, when those bad memories come pouring through my mind, I recall the cupcake, and the bad images fall away.

My mother was able to stay in her home until the day she died. I crossed the border of my pain and walked with her all the way. God gave me the strength and love to do so.

New Beginnings

Meanwhile, Jeanne had asked if we would come back and live at the cottage and be caretakers for Mark.

"Oh, yes!" I said immediately, not knowing how we could make it happen. What would we do with our home in Prospect?

But then our oldest son called and asked if he could rent our home.

"Oh, yes!" I said again, without considering any of the logistics. All I could think of was the cottage's beautiful walls of windows overlooking the forest.

A second call from our son sealed the deal. "Actually," he said, "we would like to buy your house."

Like every time before, when God opened a door, He closed another.

In one weekend, we moved from our home in Prospect to the Jenny Creek cottage and never looked back. We enjoyed nearly seven years of glorious healing in the wilderness. Wilderness has always been my place of healing, and walking that sacred ground day after day, night after night, strengthened my soul.

Our job as Secret Agents is to stay alert so that when God calls us to something, no matter how impossible it might seem, we show up and persevere in crossing whatever border or obstacle is in front of us. Whatever God does at that point is up to Him. I learned that piece of advice in 1995 when I crossed the border into China.

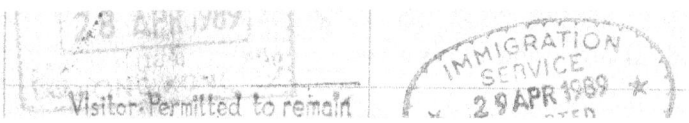

SECRET MISSION: CROSSING BORDERS

1. What impossible thing has God asked you to do?

2. What holds you back from doing that impossible thing?

China Border Crossing
1995

I traveled with a group of couriers under the direction of Don, a man I had come to highly respect after a long trip through Far East Russia and Siberia.

"Our job is to show up at the border with Bibles," he said. "The rest is up to God."

I took comfort in those words. It wasn't about how well I performed. It was about trusting God.

My teammate, Diana, and I had prayed through the night and into the morning of our border crossing. We felt confident God would lead us. We walked past the X-ray machine as planned, as though we knew what we were doing. Two other members of our group walked alongside us. Surely God would close the eyes of the guards so we could pass through and deliver the Bibles to those who wanted them so badly.

But a border guard grabbed Diana and me and shoved us to a table where he demanded our passports. His face turned red with anger as he shouted. Everyone who passed by stared—part of his way of humiliating us.

"We've brought free gifts for our Chinese friends," I said with a smile.

"This is not your country!" the guard spat.

Complete peace wrapped around me. I knew Holy Spirit was in control. I had shown up. Now, the rest was up to Him to get me safely across the border. So, I remained calm and continued to smile.

"I take your visa!" the guard shouted while pointing at my chest.

"You can't do that!" Diana shouted back.

I turned and stared at Diana, a more seasoned Bible courier than I. She knew the guard could revoke our visas if he wanted. I was shocked to see anger on her face. While I stared at her, three members of our group walked by behind her, totally undetected.

That's why we are here, so they could get through. The thought gave me comfort to know God was truly in control.

I turned back to the guard. "American newspapers say it is legal to bring Bibles to China."

"Legal, but forbidden," the guard said. Then he stormed away, leaving us sitting there, unable to do anything without passports.

After an hour passed, he returned with our bags now empty of Bibles. He also had broken the wheels on my luggage.

I smiled and said, "Thank you. I'm sorry you didn't appreciate our gifts."

He glared at me, but after several minutes he returned our passports.

When we gathered that night as a group, we discussed the day's activities. Many miracles had happened. As a team, we had reached our destination with hundreds of Bibles despite what Diana and I had lost. We met with Pastor Lamb, an amazing follower of God. He immediately turned over the Bibles to a young man who had traveled many days from northern China to Guangzhou, which is about as far away as one can go from where he started.

The young man began the journey with enough money to buy Bibles and several train tickets to make it all the way. The people of his underground church, who had raised the money and sent him, all waited anxiously. But he had been robbed on the first leg of his train trip and walked the rest of the way. Though he no longer had money to buy Bibles, he believed God would honor him for his obedience.

His face shone as we loaded him up with our bags of Bibles and gave him money for a taxi and a train trip home. After he left, we sat with Pastor Lamb, who shared his story of how he had been imprisoned for twenty-seven years because he would not deny his faith in God. His words of encouragement impact me to this day.

But that night, as we talked together, Don kept asking us what had gone wrong. "Did you pray? How long did you pray?"

"Of course, we prayed," Diana said, "but Sandy went to sleep for a while."

The room grew silent. All eyes turned toward me.

Was it my fault? Was I the reason we got caught? Should I have prayed harder or longer? I remained silent, asking God for wisdom.

Finally, I turned to Don. "You said our job was to show up, and God would do the rest? Did you mean that or not?"

The room remained silent.

Later, on the last day of our trip—after many border crossings into China and Vietnam, after seeing countless miracles, and after Don had returned to America—the rest of us decided to do one more border crossing.

"I'm going by myself," I said. "The rest of you don't want to be anywhere near me, because I have something to work out with God."

They reluctantly agreed although Diana tried to talk me out of it.

"If I get caught," I said, "you guys keep going."

That statement caused a great deal of arguing, but I finally convinced them. I waited until the team was safely through before I began my trek.

"I have to know this is You," I told God. "I have to know You were in it when Diana and I got caught. I'm going the most difficult way possible. If You were in it when we got caught, then You take me through now. If I get caught now, I'll know the problem was with me."

My words may not seem like a big statement, but this became a turning point for me. I needed to know with absolute surety that I could hear the voice of God. The outcome would affect my entire future.

I returned to the same border checkpoint where Diana and I had been caught. The same guard, who had detained us, stood by a back wall talking with another guard. Three girls worked at the X-ray terminal. I faced an impossible situation. I just knew the guard would turn around at any second and see me.

I lifted my two bags, one at a time, and plunked them on the conveyer belt. Then I walked to the other side of the X-ray machine to pick them up.

The three girls talked together animatedly. They never once glanced at the monitor.

When I picked up my bags, they looked up. My heart thumped wildly, but I flashed them a big smile. They smiled back and returned to their conversation. The guard was still facing the other way as I turned to walk out. When I stepped into the bright sunlight of China, it was all I could do not to shout for joy!

God often leads us into impossible situations. We stand at the border, knowing we can go no farther unless He does the miraculous. When our awesome Creator Redeemer opens the way for us to cross borders, we Secret Agents go out with joy and are led forth with peace. The mountains and the hills sing before us! (See Isaiah 55:12.)

Flower of Hope by SCat (Sandy Cathcart)

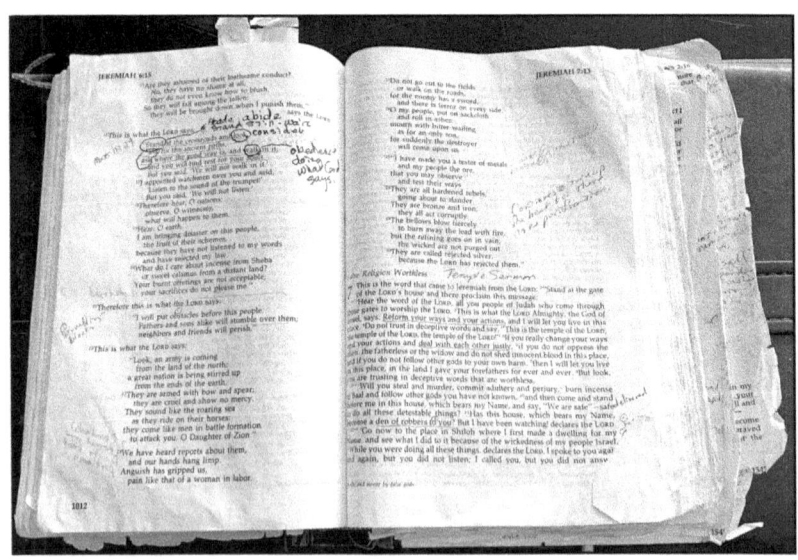

Sacred Writings (Bible).

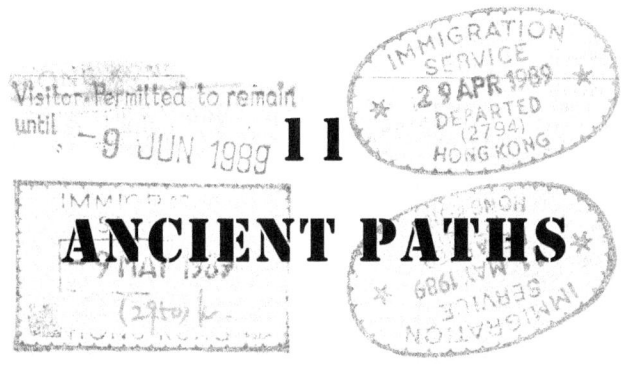

11
ANCIENT PATHS

> ... Stand at the crossroads and look;
> ask for the ancient paths,
> ask where the good way is, and walk in it,
> and you will find rest for your souls ...
> —*Jeremiah 6:16*

Eagle Point, Oregon
September 10, 2020

I'VE BEEN UP SINCE 3:00 A.M. praying for everyone I can think of. Fires rage south, east, west, and north, blocking nearly every road out of our valley. One fire took out an enormous chunk of the towns of Phoenix and Talent. Another fire burns within three miles of our town. Smoke blocks every trace of the sun.

My cousin Kim lost her home with everything in it. Her son was able to save only one of their two cats. The lloss for so many breaks my heart. Friends in the nearby city of Shady Cove had to evacuate. More fires are springing up in strange places due to a lack of rain and strong winds. Arson is suspected.

As I pray for my friends, I am struck by the fact that God cares about my friends more than I do. He also can see the future where we cannot. What does He know that we don't? What could possibly be worth all this loss?

I think back through our losses. What did we gain? What did we learn?

I rise silently and make my way through the dark, trying not to wake Cat. Then I sit and pray and write the following poem:

In 2020, COVID-19 came wreaking havoc around the globe.
People had to close themselves inside
and lost most of their hope.

At first people relished the silence.
But then many turned to violence.
And it wasn't long before they made excuses to get outside.

Some went to the streets in protest.
Others protested the protest
until riots and chaos filled our lives.

Others went to the wilderness and found God alive and well,
a creation teeming with evidence
and soul food to nourish themselves.

Then disaster after disaster blew across the land.
Cities fell one by one.
People began giving a hand.

We discovered we really liked one another.
We helped every woman, child, and man.

Forgotten was the virus.
Forgotten was the hate.
Forgotten were all the things that made love come late.

Everything that could be shaken was shaken.
What could not be shaken remained.
That's when the Great Restoration came
Built on the foundation that would never be the same.

And God wiped all our tears away.

The words of my poem depict the tragedies we have faced in this tumultuous year, but they also reflect the hope of a future beyond all the pain and hate and wrongness. Like the elves and humans waiting in the cave for Gandalf in *The Lord of the Rings*, we, too, await our coming Savior and King. A day is coming when all will be made right.

For now, we can return to the words of God given to us in the Bible. And I do so now, turning the pages to the Gospel of John where Cat and I, along with our granddaughter Rachel and her husband, Nick, and mother, Jocelyn, have been reading and studying.

I am amazed how much the situation in Jesus' day was similar to the days in which I live. Jesus healed hundreds of people, and yet they argued about whether He healed as the Son of God (as He stated repeatedly) or whether He was possessed by a demon. There wasn't any middle ground. People stood on one side or the other.

His own people were hoping He had come to save them from Roman rule, but He had come to save the world!

During this election year, people are taking sides. Even many Christians align with a man. It seems we are as guilty as the people of Jesus' day. We want God to save our country, but He is out to save the world.

And yet . . .

God is allowing fires to rage throughout the west coast, a virus is attacking at will, and people are rioting while the suicide rate is growing. How is that saving the world?

Yes, our world is broken. It has been broken from the time sin first entered the garden. It doesn't take much of a trip back through history to see how far short we have fallen in loving one another. We have thought of all kinds of horrendous ways of killing off anyone who doesn't fit into our view of what is lovely and good.

Perhaps, as my poem says, everything is being shaken so that we will finally realize what is truly important.

Pastor Rick Booye asked himself who he would be if he removed all the labels. If he wasn't a father, or a husband, or a pastor, or a teacher . . . how far down could he strip the labels? He decided that he would end up being a Christian man, that "Christian" was the one label he could never remove.

For me, I cannot remove the label, "Cat's wife." If death should separate us, I will still be Cat's wife. Into eternity, I will still be Cat's wife. We believe our love is that strong. Yet, I can say, "I am a Christian woman." I don't like using the word "Christian" these days, because it doesn't hold the same meaning as it first did. The term should signify that I am a follower of Christ, that I walk the Jesus Way.

These days, westerners seem to align the word "Christian" with being a Republican or a bigot or a racist, or a name-caller, just the opposite of being a follower of Christ. Christ was none of these. The only time we see Him angry in the Sacred Writings (Bible) is with religious people who no longer had a relationship with the Living God. They spoke the right things, but they didn't live the right things.

Are we guilty of claiming a relationship we no longer have?

If so, there is good news! God cares enough to send a warning and a way out.

As I continue reading in the Gospel of John, I see that Jesus went to the cross. He did not save His people from Rome. He didn't promise to do so. He actually promised them (and us) that we would have trouble in this world. Yet, He also told us to be of good cheer despite it all.

Really? And just how am I supposed to do that?

As soon as I ask the question, I know the answer: by focusing on the One who spoke those words. He is still out to save the world.

We can be a part of that great saving of the world even as our brothers and sisters were in the years following the death and Resurrection of Christ. Many of them gave their lives to the death. They did that out of love. That love came from the Holy Spirit living in them.

That same Holy Spirit also lives in me. And He lives in you, if you have placed your faith in Christ.

Christ did not stay in the grave. He rose! More than five hundred people saw Him taken up into Heaven. And in the same way, He will return. Indeed, great news!

I return to prayer and thank God for all the people who have reached out to help the fire victims and the many people who have contacted us to see if we are okay.

There is hope.

There is love.

We Secret Agents *can* focus on the good things and, in the rebuilding, we also can restore love to a broken world.

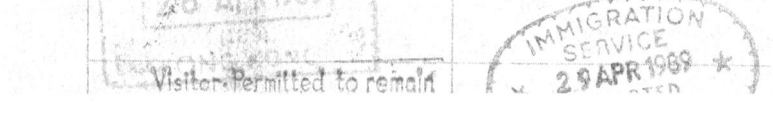

SECRET MISSION: SEARCHING ANCIENT PATHS

1. Does a favorite verse resonate with your heart? If not, ask God to give you one, then read the Sacred Writings (Bible) until one stands out to you in a big way.

2. Who in your life (past and present) do you consider heroes of faith you can emulate? If you don't have someone, ask God to show you heroes of faith from your life and the Sacred Writings (Bible).

Many heroes have influenced my life and led me back to restoration. George MacDonald, George Müller, Corrie ten Boom, and Lettie Cowman are just a few.

I learned about the sovereignty of God by reading about the life of George Müller. He was such an amazing man. He is credited with caring for more than ten thousand orphans. Not just caring for them but caring for them in such a way as to raise their standard of living above that of a poor person. The 117 schools he established provided Christian education to more than 120,000 students. He did all of this (and more!) without ever once asking for donations.

While reading about his life, our family was going through tough financial times. Our dream home in the country had burned to the ground. We had no insurance and less than ten dollars in the bank. Cat had been diagnosed with rheumatoid arthritis and could only find seasonal and part-time jobs. Our children received free lunches at school, so Cat and I held ourselves to two meals a day.

Still, the day came when I placed our last meal on the table. "That's it," I said. "I have no more beans, no flour, nothing to make another meal, and I have no money to buy anything more."

Our five children looked at me wide-eyed, but Cat remained unruffled. "Let's bow our heads."

We all joined hands while Cat asked God to supply.

I was silently pleading with God. "Please! Do a miracle like you so often did with George Müller. We are trusting you to provide for us."

We had told no one of our impending doom. Only God knew our circumstances, because we were putting God and our faith to the test. Would God provide?

He had provided for George Müller, but Müller was a great man of faith. My faith felt weak and small in comparison.

I reminded God that Jesus had said we only needed faith as small as a mustard seed. "I've got that. I have just enough faith to call on you."

Cat said, "Amen."

The phone immediately rang. A friend called to ask if Cat could row his riverboat the next day. "You and I can take turns," he said. "You can fish with my clients when you're not rowing, and you can keep whatever you catch."

Cat returned home with five enormous salmon.

I was so excited. Then I went out to the garden and discovered my peas and potatoes were ready for harvest. They had never ripened at the same time before. That made me even more excited, so I invited some friends to join us for dinner. Debbie brought a huge fruit salad and refused to take the leftovers with her.

For a week, we ate like kings! Even our kids remarked that it seemed a lot like God providing manna for the children of Israel when they were in the desert. I saw the similarities, but I also saw myself in the complainers. I would have liked to save some of that delicious salmon for future meals. But it was not to be. We ate salmon until we were again down to the last meal.

Again, we joined hands while Cat prayed. At the end of the prayer, we all stared at the wall phone, but it never rang.

Our faith was a bit stronger this time. We all expected God to do something.

As I cleaned the kitchen, our kids began whooping in the living room. I entered to discover Mike Broyles, our youth pastor, coming through the door with a box of groceries.

"There's more in the car," Mike said. "Can I get a hand?"

He received ten hands as all five kids ran out to help.

His arrival felt like Christmas. The boxes contained food, toilet paper, socks, and even some small gifts for our kids. They were having a great time sifting through to see what all was inside.

I pointed at Cat, and he pointed back at me. We both shook our heads. Neither of us had said a word about our situation.

"We were down to our last meal," I told Mike. "How did you know?"

"I didn't know," Mike said. "This is our way of saying thanks to your family for all the volunteer work you do for our church."

Those experiences were just the beginning of many miracles God did to bring our family through some very tough times. Soon after, Cat declared he was healed of arthritis and accepted a job the doctor had said he would never be able to do. Cat worked that job for thirty-two years until the day he retired.

Corrie ten Boom gave me faith to believe God could use one lone woman to change the world. Her life proved that very thing.

The writings of Lettie Cowman still touch my life today. She knew what it was like to leave community life to care for a beloved husband in isolation. God used all these people far into old age, which means He can still use me. I am still a green tree. I can bear lasting fruit.

The beauty of walking the Ancient Path toward restoration is that we never walk it alone. We have the sure witness of those who have gone before. They already have walked through the darkness and have seen a great Light ahead of them. If we listen carefully while walking those dark paths, we will hear their voices calling for us to follow.

We cannot talk about ancient paths without pointing out heroes of the faith from the Sacred Writings (Bible):

- Abraham answered the call of God to leave his home and country for a land he knew nothing about. (See Genesis 12:1-5.)

- Joseph trusted the dream God gave him, not only through good times but through dark seasons of betrayal, false accusations, and prison. (See Genesis 37 and 39-41.)

- Job relentlessly begged for an answer from God, but then when he saw his Redeemer face-to-face, he didn't have one question, saying instead, "Surely I spoke of things I did not understand, things too wonderful for me to know." (See Job 42:1-6.)

- David refused to take matters into his own hands when he had the chance to kill his brutal enemy, Saul. He trusted God had a better plan, saying, "And may the LORD avenge the wrongs you have done to me, but my hand will not touch you." (See 1 Samuel 24:12.)

- Elijah, exhausted and sore of mind, met God in the wilderness. (See 1 Kings 19:1-18.)

- The woman at the well gained faith enough to change her life and the life of everyone around her. (See John 4:1-42.)

- Peter, broken and alone after his betrayal of Christ, was restored by Jesus, Himself. (See John 21:15-25.)

Hebrews 11 gives us a list of people who have walked the ancient paths. The chapter ends by saying, "These were all commended for their faith, yet none of them received what had been promised. God had planned something better for us so that only together with us would they be made perfect."

Here is something I wrote right after coming to faith in Christ:

*Our sons had a Bible they received from Sunday School.
I took it to a place in the sun
and read the entire Gospel of John.
By the end, I absolutely knew God was real.
These men who had followed Him
would not have given their lives to the death
unless He had been who He said He was ... the Son of God.*

Looking at the lives of those who have gone before gives us the tstrength to face today and a sure hope of future redemption. The ancient paths are well-traveled and worn as we Secret Agents lead ourselves and others into restoration.

Cobby Shadley in Chiloquin, Oregon.

12
LOVE SONG

> I will sing to the LORD all my life;
> I will sing praise to my God
> as long as I live.
> —*Psalm 104:33*

Hoopa, California
Early 1980s

CHUCK SMOKER AND I had little in common with him being raised on Hoopa Valley Reservation in Northern California and me being the daughter of a migrant worker who traveled up and down the West Coast. I was never in one place very long while Chuck grew up surrounded by the same mountains and friends.

Chuck loved western music. I loved folk. Music is what first drew us together. We both played guitar, and he loved my songs.

One time, he invited me to join him and a team of friends who loved Jesus to come with him to Hoopa. We entered a big tent meeting with hundreds of people filling the entire space.

Chuck pointed and said, "See that guy there? He gave me this scar." Then he pointed to another. "He gave me this other scar."

I had never really noticed how many scars Chuck had before that night!

I was torn between wanting to stick close to him and being nervous about that being the right thing to do. What if some of these guys still wanted to get him?

We somehow made it through the night with no mishaps. I was thankful to be there when Chuck's sister, Linda Smoker, sat at the piano and belted out songs worthy of Mahalia Jackson.

That night, I slept on the couch in Chuck's mom's house. Although, I didn't get much sleep. Instead, I listened to Chuck's sister pour her heart out to God as she played her mother's piano across the room from me, a scene I will never forget. Chuck's mom, Mary Smoker, lived in Weitchpec on the side of a steep mountain overlooking the Trinity River. She was not a young woman, but she ran up and down that mountain, collecting chicken eggs and cultivating a garden as if half her age.

Seeing how Chuck grew up made me appreciate the times a friend and I walked Chuck off a drunk so he could join us to sing his songs about Jesus. Eventually, Chuck was able to leave the drinking behind, but I'm glad we shared our early days of walking with God.

His conversion experience is one of my favorites. As I recall it, he thought he had nothing left to live for. He drove out to Dead Indian Memorial Road to take his life.

One of the things I learned from Chuck is that Native Americans usually have a great sense of humor. Even when he was going to take his life, he saw the irony and humor of doing so on Dead Indian Memorial Road.

But his Creator God reached down and touched him in such a way he chose life. He pulled out his guitar to sing his thanks to God. He didn't know any Christian songs, so he sang "I Can See Clearly Now," which Johnny Nash made popular. To this day, the song is Christian to me because of Chuck's story.

Applegate Christian Fellowship
Early 1980s

Chuck and I also share a love for running. We both trained for the Pear Blossom Run every year by taking advantage of a YMCA membership. After our workouts, Cat would join us for lunch. One day, Jon Courson, the pastor of Applegate Christian Fellowship, came into the workout room. I had heard of the fellowship and was awed by the stories of hundreds of young people joining together to worship God.

Jon slapped Chuck on the back as macho guys do. "Come and sing on Wednesday night."

"Sure thing," Chuck said, then he introduced me. "Sandy writes songs and sings too. You should have her come."

"Is that right?" Jon smiled at me. "You come too."

I couldn't believe it. I attended a small church where the pastor was always nervous about me singing my songs. He had to check out my words to make sure they were theologically sound. I didn't know anything about theology at the time, but my words always passed his inspection. Jon knew nothing about me. Yet, because Chuck recommended me, he was willing to take a chance.

Our church ran about ten people on a Wednesday night, so I figured Applegate might have fifty to a hundred people. Nothing prepared me for the reality.

First, I drove fifteen miles across country roads to reach the fellowship's remote location. If I thought that might discourage people from attending, I was wrong. The fellowship was meeting in a former grocery store at the time. I arrived late because of having to park so far away. People were lined up outside along the windows and open doors. When they saw my guitar, they moved aside and waved me in.

The sanctuary was absolutely packed, yet people waved me right up to the front of the church on the second story. With all the exuberant singing, I thought maybe we would fall straight through the floor. At first, I was frightened, but then I got caught up in the worship.

We had no overhead projector or hymnbooks, yet everybody sang their hearts out. The songs were simple enough I could pick them up quickly. I kept my eyes closed, because it felt like I had been transferred to Heaven. It sounded as if thousands of angels were singing with us.

Love Song

At the end of worship, Pastor Jon called several people up to sing. Chuck was one of them. All these singers were much better than me. Yet, I felt no fear. I was the last one Jon called. When I stood on that small platform and looked out on all those faces hungry to draw close to God, I felt as if I had finally come home.

The crowd grew utterly silent as I shared my song. The connection was immediate and binding. Only later did someone call the experience what it was. God had given me an anointing for these people and this time and place. Jon called me back that weekend and the next Wednesday and the following weekend.

Then I received a call from Jeff Bates, the main worship leader. "I want to meet with you," he said. "I think you should be a worship leader with me."

"Oh no! I can't do that."

"Why not?"

"I can only sing alto. You need someone who can sing the melody."

"I'll lower the songs."

Would he really do that for me?

I thought back to my meeting with Oregon's Amazing Miracle, Thomas Welch. I had been floundering at the time, wondering if God could use me, a young mother living off grid in the hills of Southern Oregon. At the time, I was singing with Senior Citizens for Christ, even though I wasn't yet thirty. Thomas was a friend of one of the members and joined us for dessert. I had heard him before when *The 700 Club* featured him on the radio. The program was pre-recorded, yet Thomas had seen and described me from several thousand miles away. That incident set fire to my newfound faith.

Then, when I met Thomas at the Senior Citizens gathering, he stopped talking with someone else, looked at me, and said, "God is going to use your singing in a big way."

"I know," I said, which surprised me, because I didn't know it until that moment.

Now, talking with Jeff, I wondered if this was the opportunity Thomas had been talking about.

"Just meet with me," Jeff said. "Then let's go from there."

I met with him that week. Instead of singing, we spent the entire time talking. It was so much fun. Cat worked nights and slept during the day. As a mother of five young children, I was hungry to share God-talk with a peer. Even though Jeff was nearly young enough to be my son, we felt an immediate bond. Almost as an afterthought, we finally sang a song. I had never heard it before, so we had to sing it several times. Jeff sent me home with instructions to memorize the song and return to learn more.

Many women thanked me during the next few months. The songs had always been too high for them. Now, they could sing along.

I had found a group of people who loved God and loved me. For the first time in my life, I belonged. I truly had come home.

For more than a decade, Jeff and I led worship together at a time when young hearts were searching for something beyond this realm. We found what we were searching for in the person of Jesus Christ. The same love song flowed through all our hearts.

Chiloquin, Oregon
Early 1980s

Cobby Shadley and I met back in the seventies when I was a cute bartender, and he appointed himself as my personal bodyguard. I called upon my sprinkling of Cherokee blood back in those days and was grateful to call this handsome Klamath Native American my friend. He did, indeed, save me from more than one barroom brawl that would have torn up the tavern. With just a look, he could stop the meanest of drunks.

I loved it when he shared photos of himself dancing in feathers. I learned a lot about Native life from him. But I didn't learn until many years later that Cobby was different with me than he was with anyone else.

One day, talking with his brother, Cal, I said, "Cobby was always so quiet."

"Quiet?" Cal looked at me incredulously. "He was anything but quiet."

Cal went on to tell stories of how he would go to downtown Klamath on a weekend night and hear a great ruckus from The Bonanza Room. He and his friend would walk right on by, because they knew Cobby was inside causing a tremendous brawl.

"He was always quiet with me," I insisted.

Cat came into my life during that time, and the three of us became good friends. I lost track of Cobby when Cat and I moved away. More than a decade later, I rode in the back of a car heading to Chiloquin with a copy of my first book, *Songs in the Night*.

Jeff Bates was driving the car, with his wife, Gina, beside him.

I told them how I believed God would connect me with Cobby this night. I planned to give him the book. I was hoping something in my story would ignite a desire in him to know God. "I don't even know his last name, but how many Cobby's can there be?"

Jeff shook his head, but he was as excited as I was. We had seen God do so many miracles during our years together. I believed God had placed this mission on my heart. Yet, at the same time, it seemed impossible and silly.

We arrived at the home of Don and Mary Gentry just before nightfall. The intoxicating aroma of cooking wild game made us all hungry. Mary gave us a tour and said we would eat following the meeting.

"Do you know anyone named Cobby?" I asked Mary.

A quiet woman with dark, intelligent eyes, her head jerked in my direction. "Yes, I do," she said. "My brother." Then, upon seeing the excitement on my face, she added, "But he is not a Christian."

I explained to her what I hoped to do.

"Cobby has been in prison since you've seen him." She shook her head. "I rarely see him, and he certainly won't be here tonight. He doesn't even like being around Christians."

I still believed God was in this whole situation. It was too much of a coincidence that we were in Cobby's sister's house. Yet, the door seemed to have been slammed shut. I tried to push the dilemma to the back of my mind while Jeff and I led worship.

When Jon began to share the Scriptures, the garage door rumbled open behind us, and someone entered the kitchen on the other side of the living room wall. My heart began to pound. We couldn't see into the kitchen, but I just *knew* Cobby had entered.

When Jon ended with a closing prayer, my heart was beating a hundred miles an hour. I walked into the kitchen.

There he was! He was helping himself to the venison stew.

I recognized him immediately, but he had no idea who I was. Even after I told him, he didn't remember.

I was baffled. Why would God put Cobby on my heart, bring me here, and bring Cobby here, and then Cobby did not remember me? It made no sense.

Chattering people crowded into the kitchen, filling their plates and sharing conversation. Cobby and I were the only silent ones. He sat at the kitchen bar facing me but not looking at me. I leaned against the far counter, watching him out of the corner of my eye and pleading with God for direction.

Cobby seemed to pay me no mind at all. Finally, he looked up and said, "There was a woman . . . but she was married to a cop."

I had forgotten I was still married to my first husband at the time. He had moved out without filing for a divorce. Then Cat and I got together. "Yes!' I said, "that's me."

For the next forty-five minutes, I shared how Cat and I had found God and what had happened in our lives since we first met Cobby.

He listened intently, then he shook his head. "Imagine that," he said, "You meet a girl in a bar . . . and then ten years later she turns up at your sister's house . . . a Christian!"

Cat and I prayed regularly for Cobby, but I didn't see him for another decade. While I was being introduced as a teacher for First Nations Institute in Chiloquin, I spotted Cobby sitting in the audience. Afterward, Cat and I talked with him and discovered he was walking the Jesus Way. Not only that, but nearly all of his family were too.

Cobby and his family are now dear friends of ours. We pray for one another, eat meals together, and share ministry. They call me their scribe, as I record their dances and music and teachings in word and photos. It has been one of my biggest joys to be a part of their family.

Love Song

Natives are notorious for losing track of time, but I'm the worst. Cobby's brother, Cal, used to joke that I could even make an Indian tap his toe. Cal had to wait for me week after week when he drove me to Chiloquin to teach writing at First Nations Institute. I learned a lot about Native thinking and life on those long drives.

When Cal danced, he wore the regalia of a dog soldier. Back in their warring days, dog soldiers staked themselves to the earth and fought to the death, so their loved ones could reach safety. More than 500 eagle feathers made up Cal's headdress, one for each tribe in North America. When Cal danced, he was sending up prayers for all the tribes. I love the way Native Americans who walk the Jesus Way dance their prayers.

When Cal walked on to be with his Creator, his wife, Diana, and I—along with Cal's mother, Laura Grabner—put together a 365-day devotional compiled from Cal's journal entries and his favorite Scriptures written the way he would have shared them. Compiling *Eagle People Journal* is one of the most fulfilling things I have ever done. Cal's words still bless me to this day.

Cal is now known as Ghostdancer, because in his last days, he kept singing Bill Miller's song, "Ghostdance," with his arms raised to the heavens—his anthem of love to his Savior. What better way for a Secret Agent to return home to his Master?

SECRET MISSION: SINGING A LOVE SONG

1. In what ways are you showing love to the people closest to you (husband/wife, children, siblings, coworkers)? Are you speaking their love language? In other words, have you asked them what kinds of actions make them feel loved?

2. What one thing can you do today to show the love of Jesus to someone? Ask God to show you ways and people to love.

The Jesus Movement

The Jesus Movement was like a mighty wind blowing through the land, touching the hearts and souls of a generation of young people whose dreams and hopes had been trampled. It blew through city streets, catching the homeless and drug addicts and even those of us who were living off grid, deep in the mountains, looking for a better way.

All our heroes had been killed... John F. Kennedy, Martin Luther King, Jr., Bobbie Kennedy. We turned to free love, but many of us discovered that each act took a piece of our souls. We turned to drugs, only to discover (often too late) they demanded too high a price. Singers belted out songs that spoke for all of us but seldom spoke of any hope.

That's when the Spirit Wind blew through.

The Wind caught singers like Barry McGuire, Phil Keaggy, Paul Stokey, and Keith Green and groups like The 2nd Chapter of Acts and Love Song. They sang words that spoke to the depths of our souls.

The Wind caught Cat and me when we lived in the middle of the wilderness. We looked around and saw that all things worked together perfectly. Animals and birds found everything they needed at just the right time. Sun, moon, and stars proclaimed the work of an awesome Creator.

The word "Christian" meant something different in those days—a returning to a lifestyle more like that of the early church in the book of Acts. Miracles became commonplace. Drug addicts were healed instantly with no withdrawals or side effects. Hearts and dreams were restored. Love reigned supreme, no longer relegated to a sex act but encompassing people from all nations and walks of life.

Suddenly, we Secret Agents were all singing the same song—a love song that continues to this day and will continue into eternity for all who have ears to hear.

Sandy at Wilderness Trails camp.

13
LOST

> My people have been lost sheep;
> their shepherds have led them astray
> and caused them to roam on the mountains.
> They wandered over mountain and hill
> and forgot their own resting place.
>
> —*Jeremiah 50:6*

Eagle Point
November 2020

TODAY, I RECEIVED A NOTICE that our governor plans to put us on a two-week lockdown starting this coming Wednesday. I rushed to our local Walmart to grab necessary things (such as toilet paper) before the crowds emptied the shelves.

As I entered the store, a woman wrestled with a man in a wheelchair. He was clearly in a state of confused cognition. I wondered if he was her husband and how long he had suffered from dementia. Would her struggle be mine in a few years?

Quickly, I put the thought aside. I told myself, "I will trust God and not be afraid,"

In the vegetable aisle, I saw the woman again. Up closer, I realized the man was probably her son. Her husband walked behind her. I had certainly interpreted her story wrong.

Of course, we all wore masks. I find it difficult to recognize people without seeing their whole face, but she recognized me immediately, probably because of my ever-present headband.

"Hi, Sandy," she said. Then she turned to her husband. "This is the girl who was always getting lost when we were in Italy."

My constant headband gave me away, but I hadn't recognized her because of the mask. We talked for a while, then I grabbed a pack of toilet paper and headed home, thinking of that fateful trip to Italy.

Italy
1995

I was the oddball in a group of more than thirty people, who were mostly going on a dream vacation. For me, the journey was business and school related. I was researching for my current novel and earning college credit for my art and church history courses. To raise enough money for the trip, I had picked up soda cans along the highway and cleaned house for a friend.

While others enjoyed relaxing evenings in their hotel rooms during the trip, I was completing homework, organizing photos, and compiling my research.

I made very little time for sleep and ran at full speed, not wanting to miss out on a single opportunity.

Because our group was so large, the leaders split us into two groups before we toured various art galleries and places of interest. Everything was so fascinating I kept getting left behind. The result? When each group logged their final count, they figured I was with the other.

In truth, I often was engrossed with a painting or sculpture, trying to absorb every detail. How did Michelangelo create such amazing golds and blues? How was Bernini able to make stone look as soft as cloth? How did Francesco Mochi create such movement in his statue of *Saint Veronica?*

We walked where Paul the apostle and Michelangelo walked, where scores of Jewish people proclaimed they would never walk again until they were free people. We walked on top of chariot tracks carved in stone. We stood on the hillside of Assisi ,watching the same sky St. Francis watched.

My meanderings weren't a problem until we reached Milan. Our leaders planned a quick stop, so I left my main bag on the bus. I stuck my passport and twenty American dollars into my skirt pocket and grabbed my camera. The bus was parked next to a castle with towering parapets—easily found if I got separated from the group.

We toured the Brera Art Gallery in two units. I joined the first group, but the guides kept passing up amazing pieces of art. I also paused a little too long, peering through a window overlooking the National Braidense Library, where a man was turning the pages of an old book with gloved hands. I ended up at the tail end of the second group.

Then, as we passed a room without entering, I glimpsed a painting that made my heart stop—my favorite painting of Jesus by Caravaggio called *Supper at Emmaus*. It's the only painting I've seen of Jesus without a beard. Caravaggio captured the moment when the disciples first realized they were talking to Jesus after He had risen from the dead. The painting makes me wish I had been there at that moment of recognition of the risen Christ. After all had seemed lost, hope reigned once again.

As I neared the art on the far side of the empty room, I noticed differences. The disciple's arm was not foreshortened, and the basket of fruit wasn't falling off the table. The innkeeper was on the viewer's right instead of the left, and his wife stood with him. I studied the painting, noting all the marks of Caravaggio's use of dramatic light and contrast. The information provided next to the painting was all in Italian, but Caravaggio and a date of 1606 stood out. The original *Supper at Emmaus* had been painted in 1601. I snuck a photo of the tag and stared at the painting long enough to pull in every detail. I could research it later.

Suddenly, I noticed a quietness to the museum. I rushed to the hallway and didn't see another soul. I went through every room on the upper floor. Then I ran down the stairs. People lingered on the lower floor, but I didn't spot a single familiar face.

Lost

I tried asking people if they knew where my group had gone, but no one spoke English. I exited through the doors we had entered and stood on the top step. The first rule in wilderness survival is to stay at your last known location until someone returns for you.

As moments ticked by, I remembered the leaders had insisted we return in time or we would be left behind. I stood in what seemed to be an alley that smelled of diesel fuel and smog. No parapets reached above the tall buildings on every side.

Surprisingly few people came up the steps to enter the museum. Whenever they did, I said, "Castle?" and lifted my arms, palms up, in what I hoped was a universal question mark.

Finally, one woman pointed back the way she had come.

I sped through the alley and along the crowded sidewalk. Nothing seemed familiar. The roar of traffic blended with a thousand voices, adding to my panic. A crowd rushed by in every direction. The wide sidewalk went on forever. A huge expanse of street stretched between me and the far corner. Surely, I would have remembered if I had come this way before?

I stopped everyone as they passed, "Castle?"

Everyone shook their heads and kept walking until finally, one man said in perfect English. "You are very close. Keep going straight. It's at the bottom of the hill."

I nearly hugged him in response.

I ran across the wide street, causing an enormous amount of honking. Then I ran on down the hill. The bus was still parked where we left it.

"Praise God!" I said aloud. I stepped into the open door and stared into the startled face of an Asian man sitting behind the driver's wheel.

He stared back at me. He was not our driver.

"Ni hao," I greeted him.

Thankfully, he spoke Mandarin, a language I had studied. I was able to communicate enough to explain my problem.

He pointed at the empty space in front of his bus. I could only understand about every other word, but it seemed my bus had already left.

My heart sank as I remembered Matthew McAuliffe, one of our leaders, telling the rest of the team that I was a world traveler and not to worry about me. That had been back in Florence when I had set off on an adventure of my own. But that time, I had been prepared and had told him I would probably be late, and he shouldn't worry about me.

I found a nearby bench and sat down to take stock.

My options were few, and my phone battery was running low. Twenty dollars wouldn't go far if I used a hotel phone to make an international call. I dialed our church office back home. No answer.

"God!" I prayed aloud after hanging up. "I could sure use some help here."

Suddenly, I felt the urge to stand up and move. Walking at a near run, I passed the empty bus space and saw two more around the next corner and two more after that. Everything looked the same—the same parapets, the same bus parking, the same foliage. I had no way of knowing which spot was the one where I had started.

Soon, I caught a glimpse of the back of Matthew McAuliffe heading toward the castle. I hollered, "Matt!"

"Better hurry," he said. "The bus is getting ready to pull out."

We ran and jumped on board. I fell into a seat my friend Idelle Collins and her daughter Beth Erickson had waiting for me. The bus was already moving out.

"We've been praying for you," Idelle whispered. "The leaders were going to leave you behind. They said you were a world traveler and could take care of yourself."

I laughed. I wasn't feeling like such a great world traveler at that moment, but I was feeling grateful. I thanked God for my praying friends and Matt's insistence to take one more look before they left. I had come very close to being a lost traveler. From that moment on, I made sure I either had one of our leaders in view, or let them know where I was going beforehand.

SECRET MISSION: SEEKING THE LOST

1. In what ways have you been living your life as if you are on this journey alone?

2. Make a list of the people God has placed in your life. Ask God how you might reach out to them.

Wilderness Trails
Summer 2019

One of my favorite activities is volunteering with Wilderness Trails, where at-risk kids sleep in teepees during the summer and in a two-story lodge during the winter. Summer camps run for a week; winter camps run for three days. For nearly fifty years, I've been involved in some way, but for the last few years, I've been doing crafts with the girls.

I worked at both winter and summer camps until COVID-19 hit. I slept in teepees, hiked the wilderness, taught kids how to water ski, led songs and skits, and served food. I have been delighted to see many of these kids grow up into amazing adults who return to volunteer with the next generation.

Last year was the first time I helped out at a summer camp for eight- to twelve-year-old boys. I have never seen so much energy in one place. These boys, enthusiastic and excited, ran and never walked.

I was scheduled to speak at their campfire, the last event of the evening. After serving food and watching their skits, I couldn't imagine these boys sitting still enough to hear anything I would say.

I began with a few songs and told the boys they could dance along if they wanted. Then I explained how nearly every culture in the world had a special men's dance except for America. They took the challenge and danced wholeheartedly while I beat my guitar and belted out a song. If anything, they were more wired than ever as I began to speak. But an amazing thing happened. The boys went utterly silent. Their eyes never left me as I paced in front of them.

"You are not lost boys," I said, referring to a statement one child had made earlier.

"Adam is right when he said that you are found boys."

Adam Elledge, the camp leader, had explained how Jesus knew and loved every single one of them.

I showed them my paintings of lions that depicted the heart of our awesome Creator Redeemer. I held up a large painting of a lion partially hidden in the grass. You have to look hard to see Him. "This is *Lion of Judah*," I said. "He's always there even though you don't usually see Him. He always sees you."

Another painting showed a lion in motion, his mane flowing in the wind. "This one is called *Love is on the Move*," I said. "He's out to get you but not to eat you. He just wants to love you."

I held up a painting of an angry lion, snarling and ready to fight. "This is *My Defender*. You don't want to be in front of Him. You stand still behind Him while He fights the battle for you."

The boys listened in awe until I had shared every lion—*The One Who Sees, Warrior King, Compassionate One*. They were found boys, after all, and these lions depicted the heart of the One who had found them.

Many boys gave their lives to Jesus that night, and many more renewed their faith in Him. During the next few months, on Sunday mornings, when the boys came to Mountain View Christian Church for breakfast, they would hug me and tell me how they were still trusting in Jesus.

Sometimes we Secret Agents think we have found God, but the real truth is God has found us. We were the ones who were lost. Secret Agents know this and always keeps their eyes on their awesome Creator Redeemer.

Pastor Joe and wife, LeeAnn, in middle by cross.

Mountain View Christian Church, Green Springs, Oregon.

14
RESTORATION

> Though you have made me see troubles,
> many and bitter,
> you will restore my life again;
> from the depths of the earth
> you will again bring me up.
>
> —*Psalm 71:20*

Ashland Hills Conference Center, Ashland, Oregon
Fall 2019

FOR MORE THAN A YEAR, I never left Cat alone. I felt too afraid he might experience a seizure while I was away. We lived an hour from town and even farther from family, so my life became one of isolation. We had our tiny church family of about twenty people and the Wilderness Trails kids, who were an absolute delight to us, but other than that, I stuck close to home. One of my best friends lived on the same property, but I rarely saw her. I bought a Cabela's screened tent and created my first art studio. I spent many glorious hours painting more lions depicting the character of my Creator Redeemer who was always faithful, even—or perhaps I should say especially—in such a time of isolation.

Finally, the day came when I decided to attend an art dinner forty-five minutes away. Cat hadn't experienced a seizure for more than three months, so the new medicine seemed to be working. I dressed and was ready to leave when I stepped onto the porch to hug Cat goodbye. As I did so, I somehow ran into the hummingbird feeder which spilled down the back of my head. In all the commotion of making sure Cat had everything he needed I completely forgot to check my hair before I left.

I arrived at the dinner late and stood in line. No one mentioned the clump of gooey hair they must have seen. I wouldn't discover the reason for the strange looks until I returned home.

Explaining the feeling of vulnerability after being isolated for more than a year is difficult. I was excited to see my friends, but I also felt completely out of touch. Then I saw an artist friend I used to share a gallery with. Her face lit with delight. I returned her beaming smile as she headed my way. It felt so good to be wanted. I stepped out of line to welcome her hug and was met with confusion. She gave me an awkward pat and then turned to the people behind me. Her delight had been for them.

When I turned to see the recipient of all that delight, I realized he was someone I had gone to Bible School with and hadn't seen in a long time. How could I have missed that he and his wife were right behind me?

I was so wrapped up in my awkwardness that I had missed a lot of things. I ended up leaving the meeting early and fleeing home to Cat, not so much because I was worried about him (though I was), but more because I no longer belonged. The world had raced forward without me.

So many times, driving down Highway 66, I would look at Pilot Rock and think of the stories I had read of Native Americans and pioneers before me who had looked at the same rock for guidance. They all had walked on from this world, but the rock remained, steady and enduring, while we humans made a small mark.

I wondered how long my mark would last.

On that night, driving home to discover my matted hair and feeling utterly alone, I thought my mark was done. I couldn't have been more wrong.

That's the way with feelings. In my early years of following Jesus, I was told that feelings don't matter; they are neither right nor wrong. I have since learned that feelings matter a great deal, and they can be completely wrong. Feelings can lead us in a completely wrong direction. I believe it's best to not ignore our feelings. Instead, we should take them quickly to our awesome Creator Redeemer.

So, I did, and I got over my hurt quickly and moved on in the direction God was leading me. Many changes were set before me. It reminded me of a time long ago when my known world changed in little more than a heartbeat.

Applegate Valley, Oregon
Early 1990s
The Vision

I was sitting in the congregation when the Lord gave me a vision. I saw three circles, each filled with a scene. I was alone in the middle circle. My musician and singer friends were all gathered around a piano in the left circle, singing and having a great time. Jesus waited in the circle to the right, holding out His hand and asking me to join Him.

I reached my hand toward Jesus, but I kept looking back to my circle of friends. They were all having such a great time that it seemed I should be with them. When I looked back to Jesus, He was all alone. If I took His hand, it would just be the two of us.

"The choice is yours," He said. "You can go with them, or you can come with Me."

I looked back one last time, and then I took the hand of Jesus.

A New Choice

I knew that vision meant something, but nothing happened for nearly a year. Then one day, I showed up to lead worship just as I had for more than a decade and discovered I wasn't needed. That was the day my world changed. From that moment, I sat in the congregation wondering if I had done something or said something wrong. My dark thoughts took me back to the old hurt and question from hell, "If your own mother can't love you, how can you expect love from anyone else?"

I tried to give it to God—all of the questions, all of the insecurity, all the feelings of being cast aside—but the hurt refused to leave.

When New Year's came, Jeff Bates returned home from Texas and joined all the other singers on stage. I was the only one of the original group sitting in the audience.

On the way home, I couldn't say a word to my husband and children. The pain had stolen my tongue.

Then, the Lord gave me back the vision.

"The choice is yours," He said again. "Will you come with Me, or do you want to go back with them?"

I knew at that moment, if I chose my friends, I could have it all back. I could belong again. But would I feel God's anointing? Would I know His pleasure upon my life? I believed I would, but I also believed He had something better for me, something unique, if I was willing to accept it.

"I didn't know it would hurt so much," I whispered.

Cat reached over and took my hand.

Silently, I told the Lord once again that I was willing to go where He was leading.

Not long after, my car broke down. We had no money to fix it, so I ended up attending a church closer to home, one the kids and I could walk to. Nothing was expected of me there. I had two glorious years to heal. It took ten years to conquer my dark thoughts about why I had been rejected, but the day did come.

God's faithfulness is steady and true, but His timing is not at all like ours. I often call Him a Just-in-Time God, because it has been my experience that He is never in a hurry. Yet He is also never late.

Love Never Fails

Back when I was a new Christian, I read *I'm Out to Change My World* by Ann Kiemel. She was big on the fact that love, especially God's love, never fails. Both Cat and I taught that fact to teenagers in our church. One day, a young man came up to me and said, "We've been loving my sister her entire life, but she is still hooked on drugs and not changing for the better. You said love doesn't fail, but it does."

I took his hands in mine and looked deep into his eyes. "Love doesn't fail," I said, "but all too often we do."

He didn't understand what I was saying at the time, but I think he did later. We give up on loving, praying, and serving, but God never does.

"Love is patient," 1 Corinthians 13:4-8 says, ". . . Love never fails . . ."

During those ten years of wondering why I had been rejected, my love had been keeping track of wrongs. My love was looking for something in return. My love had failed.

But when I continued to take my weaknesses and feelings to Jesus, His love overpowered mine. I'm so glad it did. God had different things in mind for me than what I had in mind, and His things were much bigger and more amazing than I could have dreamed. I'm thankful that no root of bitterness has taken root to squelch the joy of that realization. I now love my past friends with genuine love, despite them hurting me so badly.

Every Secret Agent knows this kind of love is only fully realized through the Holy Spirit's power.

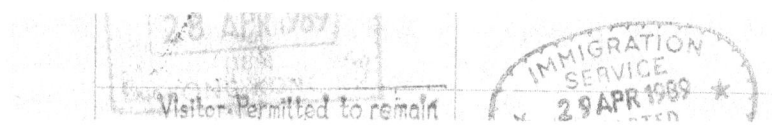

SECRET MISSION: RESTORING THE BROKEN

1. Are there people in your life you need to forgive? Ask God to bring them to mind and for His grace and mercy to allow you to forgive and love them the way He does. Continue to pray, even if it takes years, until you are able to do this.

2. In what ways do you feel broken yet set aside? Bring these things to God. Ask God for eyes to see His restoration when He brings it about. Write down the areas of restoration you already have seen in your life.

Green Springs
Fall 2013
Giving It All Up

For the next two decades, I rarely led worship anywhere. Yet, I continued to sing my songs to my awesome Creator Redeemer while I sat on the porch of our mountain home. Birds sang along with me, but no humans joined in as I wrote the words to new songs in the pages of my journal.

Like my vision, it was Jesus and me.

When Cat and I moved in one weekend to the Green Springs cottage, I left a lot of things behind. including my beloved piano and my songs. I gave the piano to my son and threw away all my songs. The cottage was much smaller than our other home, so we had to make choices. We could either have my piano or the books, but there wasn't room for both.

Cat and I both loved books. It seemed selfish to keep my piano, so I chose the books.

I think I threw away the songs more out of hurt. God knew the words. He was the only one hearing me sing those songs, so why keep them? The loss felt like a great ripping away, but I believed it might help me move forward to whatever new thing God had for me.

Remember, I was suffering from severe depression at the time.

Part of the problem stemmed from not attending church in nearly three years. I was still going to Bible School and had just received my degree before moving to the cottage, but on Sunday mornings, Cat and I stayed home.

I remember asking Cat one day, "Do we go to church anymore?"

"I don't know," he said.

We never really talked about it, and neither of us knew exactly why we quit going. It began when the pastor we loved took a sabbatical. We ended up taking a sabbatical along with him. Then when he returned, we didn't.

I think if someone had asked us why we weren't there, we would have shown up, but no one asked. In a congregation of more than two thousand people with two services on a Sunday morning, it would be hard to know if a person was missing or simply attending another service.

Mountain View Christian Church was the only church on the Green Springs. Less than five miles away from our cottage, we decided to try it. The gleaming white building featured a steeple with a church bell. The sanctuary was small, with comfortable old pews facing a cross in front of an enormous window that looked upon the forest and mountains beyond. It smelled of freshly brewed coffee.

The congregation was even smaller than the sanctuary. Less than two dozen people filled the pews.

The pastor looked more like a cowboy, decked out in boots and a beard, but his eyes were friendly as he stood to speak. He welcomed us as new people. We were both embarrassed and warmed, but it felt good to be wanted.

Instead of a sermon, Pastor Joe Johnson showed us a slideshow of Texas. He had just returned from three months of working there. We never once opened our Bibles.

Just a few years before, while I attended Bible School, one of the questions asked of us was what we would look for in a new church. I had answered that I would need good worship and good teaching. The worship at Mountain View Christian Church was good, but I found it difficult to sing along, and there had been absolutely no Bible teaching.

When Pastor Joe closed in prayer, I turned to Cat and said, "Well, that's the last time we come here."

But then Pastor Joe opened the doors to the kitchen. "Everyone is invited for coffee and food," he said. Delicious aromas of roasted meat and potatoes filled the air.

We joined them.

After spending an hour with these mountain neighbors, we were hooked. These people clearly cared about one another. I realized at that moment that we had just experienced what church is supposed to be, people loving one another.

I could access good teaching on the Internet and even sing along with wonderful worship leaders, but Mountain View Christian Church offered something different. Because it was the only church on the mountain, people came from various backgrounds. They supported one another and cared about each other even though they didn't agree on exact theology or politics. They were united in their common belief in Jesus as the Son of God.

We found ourselves looking forward to Sundays and spending time with our new family.

Mountain View Christian Church
2013
Restoration

One fall day, Pastor Joe asked if I would lead worship. Our worship leader had moved away, and Pastor Joe knew I had led worship in the past.

Three times I turned him down, but he continued to ask. "Okay," I finally said. "I'll pray about it and let you know."

I faced a few problems. I didn't have a piano, and my guitar needed repairs. Mountain View Christian Church had an amazing pianist and a keyboard player, so I decided to look for a new guitar. I would need to learn new songs, and the other musicians would have to follow me, because I wasn't accomplished enough to follow them.

At the time, I was trying to remember a song. I couldn't even recall what it was about. "Okay, Lord," I prayed, "if you give me that song, I'll know you want me to lead worship. Otherwise, I'm saying, 'No,' for the final time."

Immediately, the Lord gave me the song in its entirety.

I wrote it down and began writing down other songs the Lord brought to remembrance. I could barely keep up with the memories.

I called Pastor Joe and accepted his kind offer. He was delighted.

I began looking for a guitar. My 12-string Takamine was fixable, but it would take weeks at the repair shop. I didn't have weeks. I already was committed to the following Sunday. My Takamine had initially cost me seven hundred dollars, so I thought it might be around a thousand now, which was slightly above my budget. I was shocked to discover the price was more than two thousand dollars.

I visited another music shop and tried out guitars in my price range. None of them created the sound wanted.

Finally, the owner brought me a guitar and said, "Try this one."

I played a few bars and stopped. "This is it," I said. "I'll take it."

"It's a Taylor," he said while reaching out his hand. "It's three thousand dollars."

I gently handed the guitar back. He didn't need to say another word. He had made the point that what I was looking for was way above my budget.

I left, embarrassed and feeling as if I must have heard the Lord wrong. I was so sure He would provide a guitar, but there was only one shop left and no time to order one.

I entered the last shop and began looking at price tags. All of them exceeded my budget.

"Can I help you?" a salesman said.

I shook my head. "I doubt it." I told him what I had experienced at the music center.

He smiled. "I may have something for you. Wait here."

He went into the back room and brought out a twelve-string guitar—a Martin. The brand is known for its beautiful sound, but also for its high price.

"Give this a try," the salesman said.

I fell in love immediately. Not only did it have a great sound, but the narrow neck also perfectly fit my increasingly arthritic fingers.

"How much is it?" I was sure it was way out of my budget.

"This guitar is an experiment," he explained. "They crafted it with people like you in mind. People who love music but don't have much money. It's under seven hundred bucks."

I thought there must be a catch.

"It's the only one we have," he said. "And we aren't planning to get any more." He agreed to hold it for me overnight, but I must make up my mind by the next day.

I drove the hour-and-a-half home and looked the guitar up on the Internet. A young man had made a YouTube video of himself playing this very guitar. I loved the sound, and so did he. The next day, I drove back to town and brought the Martin home. That Sunday, I became the worship leader of Mountain View Christian Church, a privilege I enjoyed for nearly seven years.

God also provided a Kawai MP6 keyboard that fit perfectly in our small home. I began writing songs and sharing them with our community. Some of my songs became the favorites of our small congregation.

I treasured all these things in my heart. I had given it all up. All the songs. My guitar. My piano. My voice. And God had restored them all.

We Secret Agents will all experience times of brokenness, but we also have full assurance that restoration will come, . . . and not a day too late.

Box R Ranch, Green Springs, Oregon.

15
CHOSEN

> But you are a chosen people,
> a royal priesthood, a holy nation,
> God's special possession,
> that you may declare the praises of him
> who called you out of darkness into his wonderful light.
> —*1 Peter 2:9*

Eagle Point, Oregon
August 2020

For a few moments this morning, I was the leader of the pack. I didn't notice the other bikers until they were about a quarter mile behind me. I first saw the flash of a bicycle headlight in my rearview mirror. *Oh great! They're going to pass me like I'm sitting still.*

Most of the time, I don't worry about speed. At my age, it's quite an accomplishment to simply be out there doing something. I'm conquering fourteen miles, six days a week, for goodness' sake.

I was coming up over the back side of Goliath, a rise in the road I personally named. The next quarter mile was all downhill, so I poured on the speed. When I turned onto Riley Road, it looked for all the world like I was the one leading the pack. Anyone watching would think the rest of the bikers were trying to catch up with me.

The feeling of euphoria was short lived, because they all drew alongside. They were dressed in stretchy pants and helmets with all the gear available to serious cyclists. They looked lean and fit and not at all winded. I, on the other hand, wore my pink Cabela's coat and blue jeans and headband, no helmet. But for a short while, I was one of the pack.

They all said, "Good morning." They even rode beside me for a short while.

I belonged to a unique group of cyclists for those few moments. I reveled in my newfound acceptance.

They all left me behind. I drew in deep breaths of fresh-cut hay as their colors blended into one, and they became specks in the distance.

Prospect, Oregon
2003

The bicycle incident reminded me of when my granddaughter, Rachel, left me behind. At least that's what I thought had happened. She was probably seven years old, sitting at the counter watching me cook breakfast. As usual, I was making a huge mess as I cooked, and Rachel already had become a clean freak.

I tried to clean up as the cooking progressed, but it never works for me. I can either clean, or I can cook, but I definitely cannot do both simultaneously. I either end up dropping things or burning the food.

On this day, I did both. The smell of burnt toast filled the air as the clanking and clanging continued.

I turned to smile at Rachel.

She didn't smile back. Her face scrunched in thought as she said, "Grandma, I don't think I'm so weird anymore."

With a spatula in one hand and a skillet of scrambled eggs in the other, I froze. We had a special song about Grandma and Rachel being two weirdos. Was she leaving me behind for bigger and better things?

At that moment, I felt old and unloved.

Rachel's face brightened into a smile. "It's okay, Grandma," she said. "I'll still be on your team."

I released my held breath.

All my life, I felt like I was standing outside, like I didn't quite fit in.

I was an only child, while most people had at least one sibling. My family traveled from place to place during a time when most kids grew up in one town. Mom and Dad came from Arkansas and Oklahoma but raised me in the northwest. I always had (and some say I still have) a slight accent and used a lot of different words than my schoolmates. People still laugh at how I pronounce some words, such as wolf and roof.

My father never made it to high school, yet he never encountered anything he couldn't do when he set his mind to it. We didn't have a TV until I was entering high school. I came home to an empty house when most kids had stay-at-home mothers. I started cooking when I was seven years old and roamed the woods alone at the same age.

I always thought I was weird until I discovered I was an artist. For the first time, I felt like I belonged. The feeling was short-lived as my art friends moved ahead of me. I will never forget the day I painted my first lion.

Box R Ranch, Green Springs, Oregon
2007

My art friends and I were attending Masterpiece Christian Art Conference at Box R Ranch in the mountains of Southern Oregon. Frank Ordaz was one of our presenters. He is a master artist who is know for his work on the Star Wars movies.

On the first day, I discovered Frank painting by himself in one of the barns. He graciously let me watch. Surrounded by the smell of hay and horses, we talked as if we were old friends. I was excited about all the things I learned from him that day.

He told me this was his first time teaching in such a venue and confessed he was nervous. He also said he liked talking while painting. I listened while he told me about his life. Frank had been a highly successful painter since he was a toddler and is probably best known for his work with the Star Wars franchise.

I found him absolutely delightful.

Later, he gave a demonstration to the entire group. No one made a sound, and I saw a bit of shake to his hand. I remembered he liked to talk while painting, so I began asking questions. It seemed to help.

My art friends were embarrassed. They thought I was disturbing Frank.

I made the ultimate mistake when his painting fell into a phase I recognized from my own work.

"So," I said, "is this the ugly stage?"

Frank held his brush midair and laughed.

My friends all gasped and took a step back, looking at me as if I had committed the error of all time.

Chris Hopkins, another of our amazing teachers who later became a very good friend, leaned in and whispered, "You know this is his first time?"

Secret Agent

"I—I didn't mean anything bad," I stammered. "I was excited to learn the ugly stage is just part of the process."

Frank took it good naturedly and agreed. "Yes. This is the ugly stage. Hopefully, we'll get through it. The important thing is not to rush it."

The rest of the afternoon, none of my friends talked with me. I couldn't blame them. They didn't know I had spent time with Frank earlier, and he knew I was learning from him. My comment did sound rude, but he was aware I was grasping something important.

That evening, instead of eating dinner, I decided to practice what I learned from Frank. I returned to the cabin and set up my easel on the porch, determined not to rush the ugly stage. I was having so much fun!

Using a palette knife, I slapped paint onto the canvas, creating a lion hiding in the grass.

It was a work of pure joy.

I was nearing completion when my friends came up the steps and stood beside me. For a while, no one said a word while I painted. Then one said, "Have you ever thought about using less color?"

"No," I said. "I love color."

"Perhaps you should think about using a more limited pallet," another said.

"Hmmm."

A few more offered suggestions. Not a single one offered a compliment.

Finally, I lost the joy.

They all entered the cabin. My friends didn't mean to hurt me. They were simply trying to help improve my skills.

I stood before my painting, arms dropped by my sides. *Whatever made you think you could be an artist?*

I quickly finished the painting and took the whole thing, easel and all, to the far end of the porch to dry. I was embarrassed for anyone to see it. Then I joined my friends in the cabin.

No one asked how it turned out.

I sat silently while everyone talked around me. I no longer felt a part of the group. Instead, I felt outside, as if I floated in a separate universe.

A while later, one of the girl's husbands came through the kitchen door next to where my painting was drying on the porch. He hollered, "Who did the painting of the lion?"

Everyone stopped talking.

"It's awesome!" he said.

Suddenly, I knew I had painted the lion for him. And for others like him, who would love it. Not everyone would love my work and that was okay.

Today, I have a price tag of five thousand dollars on the original of that lion, because it is Cat's very favorite. I love it too, as do many other people. The print is very popular.

Medford, Oregon
2005
Upper Rogue Art Show

I could have learned the lesson earlier at my very first art contest. My art teacher had encouraged each of her students to enter two paintings. A judge critiqued each painting in front of everyone. I noticed the judge, Carl Seyboldt, a kind man, was very diplomatic. If he didn't have anything good to say about the painting, he would, instead, say something like, "I've fished there, right on that rock."

My first painting—a colorful portrait, because I especially enjoy using surprising colors—came up for review.

Carl looked at it and brought a hand up to his chin. A minute ticked by before he said, "You like color, don't you?"

My face went hot. It must have been the nicest thing he could think to say. I sat there thinking I must have failed while he went on to several other paintings.

When my next colorful portrait came up, Carl's voice brightened. "Oh! You like color!" Then he turned to me, made sure he had eye contact, and said, "Not everyone is going to like it. But keep it up! One of these days people are going to look at your work and say, 'That's one of Sandy's.'"

I'm so thankful for Carl's kind words, and I'm thankful for my awesome Creator Redeemer's patience with me. He has given me enough reminders and encouragement to keep me going.

Now, I pray for my work that hangs in people's homes and offices, that viewers will look at those paintings and be touched with the love of God. That in a moment when they are depressed, they can look up and know God cares for them and is standing with open arms.

Being on the same team does not mean we have to be the same as all the other members.

Romans 12:4-6 says it best:

For just as each of us has one body with many members,
and these members do not all have the same function,
so in Christ we, though many, form one body,
and each member belongs to all the others.
We have different gifts,
according to the grace given to each of us ...

We are each unique creations of an amazing Creator, and we each have a unique group of people we can reach out to with the gifts He has given us. I have determined to never try to be like someone else. I will take joy in what God has given me and let Him bless it and multiply it as He sees fit.

A Secret Agent knows to take joy in the process.

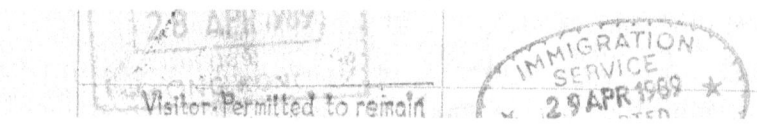

SECRET MISSION: CHOOSING ACCEPTANCE

1. What gifts has God given you? If you are not sure, ask Him to show you and/or remind you of people who may see your gifts better than you do. Ask them.

2. How are you using your gifts for God? You have a gift, or gifts, that will benefit the rest of the team. Ask God to show you what your gifts are and how best to serve others with those gifts.

When I first gave my heart to the Lord, our family of seven lived in a home that could only be reached by foot. We had no electricity, running water, or phone service. I baked pies and cookies and took them to the local mission that readily accepted my gifts. I took my guitar into nursing homes and sang to the residents. I bought Gospels of John and gave them out to people I felt would love receiving such a gift.

Then I began teaching fifth-grade girls in a Sunday School class. I had no idea how to teach the Bible, since I was just learning about it, but I followed a curriculum and taught the girls what I had learned the previous week. I taught those girls all the way up to their college years. Many of them are still my friends today.

Using your gifts can be as unique as you are. Simply pray, and then do whatever God places on your heart.

Once we give our lives to God, we become part of an amazing team. Our awesome Creator Redeemer uses us all together. Yet, He still uses us as individuals as well. He knew me before the foundation of the world. He called me to be a child of His, even knowing every wrong thing I would ever do. He knows you in the same way.

To be used by God is to realize our full potential. Nothing is more satisfying. But sometimes, the way He wants to use us is not at all what we expect.

Tonight, I was reading through an old journal of mine from a couple of years ago. Crystal Ortmann, a friend and nurse, woke in the middle of the night praying for Cat and me. Her prayers came at a much-needed time. She wrote me an email saying I may need to let go of some things.

I balked at her email. I liked my life, and I didn't want to let go of anything. Yet, her words rang true, so I took them to my Lord and asked Him to help me know what needed to go.

Since Crystal's email, I have had to let go of my home in the woods. I couldn't sleep for three nights after finding out we had to move. I also had to let go of my volunteer work with Wilderness Trails Camp, my job leading worship at Mountain View Christian Church, the greater part of my network of established friends, my church family and pastor, the Bible study I was leading, and so much more.

Letting go happened a few months earlier than the pandemic. Consequently, I was in an excellent place to be working alone when COVID-19 hit. God already had me teaching classes through Zoom meetings. I also have been able to help others move through the loss they have experienced since our lockdowns—God's way of having me comfort others with the comfort He has shown me.

I had forgotten Crystal's words until rereading them tonight. She was right in what she said. Even though I wanted to reject those words, her warning prepared my heart for what was to come. God used her to soften the pain and help me cry out to Him as I walked through that wilderness.

Southern China
1987

My awesome Creator Redeemer uses people to help me in my journey, but I love that He also uses me to help others. One of my most special connections happened on a train in China. My two friends and I had ridden hard bed from Hangzhou to Guangzhou. That means we each occupied three bunkbeds on one side of an open compartment. Four Chinese people shared the three narrow beds on the other side.

I felt such a bond with the woman on the other side, who shared one of those skinny beds with her husband. Toward the end of our trip, I wrapped a Chinese Bible in one of my bandana headbands and gave it to her. She peeked inside the bandana then clutched it to her chest. Then she pointed up and then to her heart.

She kept rocking with her eyes closed, still holding that Bible hidden in my bandana. Without being able to speak the same language, we had felt the bond of sisterhood that the Holy Spirit gives. After hiding her Bible in a safe place, she tied on my headband and never took it off the rest of the trip. I will see her in Heaven, and we will be like sisters.

I am so thankful I am part of the family of God. There is a place for me. Jesus Yeshua will never leave me behind. I am chosen, and I belong. I am one of His unique group. Yet, I also must remember not to get out ahead of Him. Things never turn out well when I do. He knows the way. He's been here before, and He also knows every danger and trap that lies ahead.

Remember those bike riders behind me after I sped down Goliath? Those bike riders had one guy leading them, probably showing them the way.

In a similar way, Jesus Yeshua leads His Secret Agents. We are chosen to be part of God's family. And just as those bike riders stuck close together playing off each other's wind channels, we Secret Agents should do the same, encouraging one another as we continue this journey called life.

Cat in the Sky Lakes Wilderness.

Steve Evans, our guide boss and friend.

16

TRACKS

> Because of the Lord's great love
> we are not consumed,
> for his compassions never fail.
> They are new every morning;
> great is your faithfulness.
> —*Lamentations 3:22-23*

Eagle Point, Oregon
November 2020

DEPRESSION HIT ME HARD YESTERDAY following a night of nightmares and not enough sleep. I forced myself to climb out of bed and dress for my bike ride. I discovered a flat front tire. No problem. I had bought a new pump earlier in the week, so fixing it should have been a piece of cake. But, no. I couldn't get the pump to work, and then the whole thing fell apart.

I placed the entire mess in Cat's hands.

That soon brought on another problem. I already was frustrated beyond help. Cat soon became as frustrated. He hadn't eaten any breakfast yet, so the timing wasn't good to stretch his mind. He was soon confused and wanted me to unconfuse him.

Of course, I ended up doing just the opposite, confusing him more. Things went downhill quickly. He shook with frustration and anger, all because I hadn't controlled my own frustration.

I laid a hand on his arm until he looked into my eyes. "This isn't worth it," I said. "Forget the bike. Let's go in the house and start over."

Cat was unable to let go of his frustration, so I went inside, made coffee, and waited.

Finally, he joined me, smelling of bicycle oil and metal. He was holding the old, broken pump in his hands. "This will work now."

But I knew it wouldn't. That's why I had bought the new one.

I placed a cup of coffee on the table in front of him. "That's the old pump."

His eyes widened as a shock wave of confusion hit him full blast. He thought he was holding the new pump. The realization undid him. He sat in the chair, staring at the pump.

I hated myself. Did I really need to point out that mistake? Why couldn't I have just let it go?

Now, both of us were frustrated again. Cat was depending on me to keep everything together; I couldn't even keep myself together.

A hundred unrelated depressing thoughts flew through my mind. This weekend was our family's annual search of the forest for a perfect Christmas tree. That would not happen this year for so many reasons. I played out every reason, depressing myself even more.

I went from those thoughts to thinking we couldn't even afford to buy a tree. That led to thoughts about how quickly Cat's retirement was running out. That led to thoughts of escalating events threatening financial ruin. Soon, I was so depressed that I just wanted out of this world.

I needed someone to pull me off the ledge.

I wondered who to call. The national hotline? As I thought out the phone scenario, I felt pretty sure they wouldn't be able to help. I probably would leave the person on the other end of the line as depressed as myself.

I sat at the kitchen table with my dark thoughts. Relentless tears ran down my face. The house was silent when a favorite song came on my playlist. The words reminded me of how I've seen the tracks of God's faithfulness all over my life.

"God. I need you," I whispered. "Please help me to think Your thoughts."

My eyes focused on the Christmas cactus sitting in front of my studio window. Always a beautiful plant, in this new home, it was thriving. An explosion of pink blossoms stretched for the sun.

I realized at that moment that I can be like that plant. I can thrive in this place God has clearly given us. I can reach out to Him at all times.

I stood and reached out for my husband.

He was quick to return my embrace, as he always is.

I whispered a prayer of thanks, and then another that Cat is doing so well, and then another that God is always faithful, and then another, and another, and another . . . an entire series of thankful prayers.

God redeemed our day. It happened in tiny increments. Then it grew until I was whole again, and Cat was back to himself.

Be Careful Little Eyes

I learned a couple of things through this event. First, I had been listening to an audiobook I should not have been. I had downloaded it because it looked like an interesting suspense story. I knew nothing of the author or what the book was about. The author turned out to be an amazing writer. I found myself unable to quit listening even after realizing the story would not have a happy ending.

That's one thing a caregiver and Secret Agent should always know. We should never knowingly add depression to our lives. We have enough to face and overcome each and every day.

The book's message and worldview were much worse than I expected. In the end, the main character takes her life. We readers were left with the idea that was a good thing. If the story had been a physical book, I would have thrown it across the room.

I am amazed how that evil thought wormed its way into my mind so that when I became frustrated about something as silly as a bicycle pump, I allowed my thoughts to go down a road until I didn't want to live anymore. If I had played different music that day, something melancholy from the past, it might have been enough to throw me completely over the edge.

What we read, what we listen to (music or books), the thoughts we allow, all make a difference in our outlook and day-to-day living. This understanding puts a whole new light on "taking every thought captive," as we are told in 2 Corinthians 10:5.

We find it easy to say, "It's just a book," or "It's just a song," or "It's just a movie." In truth, those books, songs, or movies are powerful worldview changers, as are all types of social media. Even traditional news platforms have become worldview changers. It is good to remember the truth in the children's song that reminds us, "Be careful little eyes what you see. Be careful little ears what you hear."

Taking Care

The second thing I realized is just how important it is to care for our environment. I'm not talking about forests and ecosystems, although I believe it's important to take care of those environments as well. But what about the environment we create in our homes? That environment (along with the workplace) probably influences us most.

How are we polluting those places?

As I said above, the books, movies, and music we bring into our lives can either enhance or pollute our environment. Our thoughts hold the same potential. Words are also a huge environment changer. Are we speaking words of encouragement and hope? Or are we tearing one another down with our words?

This year, 2020, was the worst word-polluting year of my entire life. I've lived through the elections of thirteen different presidents, but this year topped them all for name-calling and just plain meanness. Current election results show a horrible split among the people of our land. Many of my Christian friends have spewed the same kind of meanness and name-calling as everyone else.

Jesus said, "If you love those who love you, what credit is that to you? Even sinners love those who love them" (Luke 6:32).

How much time are we spending in the Bible where our life comes from?

The Words of the Living God are there to help us find the right path, to help us stay on that path, and to warn us when we are turning aside. If we are not in the Word, we end up acting and talking like everyone else. The life of a Christian is counterintuitive, which means without Holy Spirit leading, we most often choose the wrong way.

This week, I have received Facebook messages from many Christian friends who are leaving Facebook. They plan to go to a social media site where they can continue to share their views with one another.

How is that bringing light into a dark world?

I'm thankful for all kinds of social media, because they are vehicles where I can share and receive light. The greater part of my Christian friends shares encouragement and light on a daily basis. I choose to focus on them and not on those who say they are Christian by their words while their lives prove differently.

As Cat always tells me, "Sleeping in a garage does not make you a car."

Jesus said it like this, "A new command I give you: Love one another. As I have loved you, so you must love one another. By this everyone will know that you are my disciples, if you love one another" (John 13:34-35).

He knew how hard it would be for us to do so, yet three times in three sentences He tells us to love one another. I think He means it.

Redemption

Part of the redemption of my depressing day came through a friend who loves me in the way Jesus was talking about.

Lori Di Betta took the time to select a beautiful birthday card she knew I would love, and then she wrote a Bible verse out by hand that met my need perfectly. She sent it by U.S. mail. It arrived on the day of my greatest need. Her act of love provided the final touch of bringing me back from the edge of the cliff.

Someone cared. Not only that, God cared. And, knowing my need before it even came to be, He placed the idea on Lori's heart to send that card.

That's the amazing God we serve! I will be a Secret Agent till the end of my life because of that kind of love and faithfulness.

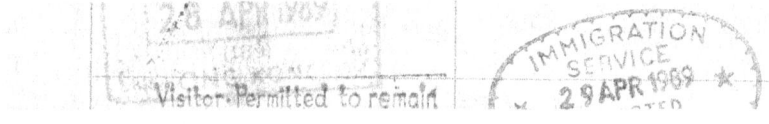

SECRET MISSION: TRACKING GOD

1. Make a list of the things God has done in your life. Ask God to help you remember any you may have forgotten. Ask God for the eyes to see where He has touched your life. Memorize or keep this list handy for when others need to hear about the tracks of God's faithfulness in your life.

2. Make a list of family and friends who could benefit from hearing about God's work in your life, and then pray for opportunities to share and the courage to do so.

Eagle Point, Oregon
December 2020
Calling Back

Dave Smith died this month.

The news of his passing shook me. He and his wife Kathy were longtime friends of ours. We had lost each other for years. Then found each other when Kathy and I were both visiting a naturopath. She was seeking help for her husband, because he was in the early stages of dementia. He seemed so much like his old amiable self that I found it hard to believe.

He stood there smiling at me while she told me about their tortured journey. His eyes appeared clear and full of humor.

"He can't talk," Kathy said. "He has aphasia dementia. But he can understand you just fine."

After listening to the story of our journey, Kathy talked me into bringing Cat to the naturopath. Although Cat's dementia was different, similarities existed. "Cat sounds like he's about three years behind Dave," she said.

Realizing that Dave was ahead of us gave me hope as long as Dave was alive. The news of his death made the end seem far too real and way too close.

This week I took a meal to Kathy with the idea of being there for her in her hour of need. The smell of warm pot roast and vegetables drifted around us as we talked.

She didn't take one bite. "It's hard to believe that just three years ago, Dave was out in the garage working on his projects."

Three years.

Suddenly, I wanted to return home to Cat. To soak up every minute possible of our short time together. Kathy loved Dave like I love Cat. She seemed lost without him. Even the house seemed empty without his presence.

"I couldn't be here when they took him." She couldn't bring herself to say the word "body."

I understood, because I was in the house alone with my mother for hours after she died. I, too, had to leave the house when the mortuary people came to pick her up.

"I ran outside," Kathy said. "I felt like I would die. But then, God gave me a vision of Dave."

She saw Dave standing in a beautiful field with myriad birds flying all around him.

He reached for one of his bird books he always used to look up the names of various species, but then he stopped. "Kathy!" he shouted. "I don't need a book. I know all the names."

He started listing them off.

"He was so happy," Kathy said. Then she told me about another vision the Lord gave her, where Dave again called her by name.

"Kathy!" Dave yelled. "There's no want here. I don't need anything!"

He was ecstatic with joy.

It meant a lot to Kathy that he called her by name. Because of the aphasia, she hadn't heard his voice in a very long time.

Her words both comforted and frightened me. I couldn't imagine facing life without Cat. The thought left my heart feeling broken and lost. But then Kathy told me something that really encouraged me.

"I think you are in the hardest part right now," she said.

She explained how difficult it was when Dave fought her at every turn. "I told him not to drive a car anymore, but he would do it anyway."

"How did you get him to stop?" I asked.

"I didn't. One day he had a small accident. Thank God no one was hurt. At first, the officer thought Dave was drunk. His words were garbled and made no sense. That put an end to his driving."

I had been thinking Cat and I were in the easy part. I reasoned that if I had such problems now, how could I be there for him when the going gets really rough?

I took courage from her words. Like Lettie Cowman's poem below, Kathy was ahead of me, calling back, "You can do it! God is faithful all the way!"

Words of life, freely spoken, and given at a time when Kathy was going through such deep pain. That's the kind of words we should all be sharing. That's why I'm sharing these words now, with the hope that you—my reader and fellow Secret Agent—will find courage and strength and hope for the days ahead.

God never promised we wouldn't go through pain. Jesus, in fact, said we would face great pain, but He also promised to be with us through it all. (See John 16:33.)

If you have gone a little way ahead of me, call back —
It will cheer my heart and help my feet along the stony track;
And if, perhaps, Faith's light is dim, because the oil is low,
Your call will guide my lagging course as wearily I go.

Call back, and tell me
that He went with you into the storm;
Call back, and say
He kept you when the forest's roots were torn;
That, when the heavens thunder
and the earthquake shook the hill,
He bore you up and held you where the lofty air was still.

O friend, call back, and tell me for I cannot see your face;
They say it glows with triumph,
and your feet sprint in the race;
But there are mists between us and my spirit eyes are dim,
And I cannot see the glory, though I long for word of Him.

> *But if you'll say He heard you*
> *when your prayer was but a cry,*
> *And if you'll say He saw you*
> *through the night's sin-darkened sky—*
> *If you have gone a little way ahead,*
> *O friend, call back—*
> *It will cheer my heart*
> *and help my feet along the stony track.*
> *—Lettie Cowman*
>
> (Streams in the Desert, *December 19, updated version*)

Not Looking Far

Today, the last day of 2020, I'm looking ahead at 2021, but I'm not looking far. Today has enough troubles of its own. So, I seek God for the courage and grace and strength to meet the needs of this day. I determine to soak up all the goodness this day has to offer and look at each moment as a gift. I determine to let go of any fear that pops up.

You can do the same, dear reader. God's tracks are all over your life as well. If we hang onto the fact that God is good all the time and that He knows the future and is bringing us to a better space, then we can trust Him in the troubles each day throws at us. You can be sad in the process. You can shed tears.

He knows. He understands the pain. His open arms are available all the time.

We all need to spend more time in His presence. There is no place our feet walk that is not a Sacred Place. Stop and turn to your faithful Creator Redeemer.

I'm hearing a lot of talk about how 2021 has to be better than 2020. I'm not seeing evidence of that. For the first time, God impressed on me that the beginning of 2021 is not actually a beginning at all but simply a continuation of what has come before. The word He gave me for this year is "perseverance."

Keeping track of what God has done in the past (as I have done in this book) reminds us that He has used a lot of things we thought were really bad to bring about some amazingly good things in our lives. Since our Creator Redeemer has been faithful in the past, we can trust that He will remain faithful in His promise of a future and hope. One day, we will live with Him in eternity where death will be but a memory and tears and sadness will be no more.

We face uncertain and tremulous times. Yet we Secret Agents can persevere by looking back and tracking the evidence of God's faithfulness all over our lives.

Stunning rainbow behind Mountain View Christian Church on our last Sunday.

View from my Eagle Point Studio.

17
AWAKE

> Awake my soul!
> Awake, harp and lyre!
> I will awaken the dawn.
> *Psalm 57:8*

Eagle Point, Oregon
January 2021

"REVIVAL IS IN THE AIR. Catch it if you can."

That's a line from one of my favorite songs. I love it, because I can sense revival on the wind, just like in the Jesus Movement. The music of the song makes me feel as if I'm flying.

Two years ago, Clay, our youngest son, invited us to Disney World for my birthday. He owns a home near the park, and our granddaughter, Tiffany, works in entertainment for Disney. My birthday comes in December, so the park was decorated for Christmas.

What a truly magical time.

One of my highlights was walking through Pandora and flying on a mountain banshee in the "Avatar Flight of Passage" ride. I have always loved the movie, *Avatar*. I often dreamed of being able to walk through those enchanted forests.

Narnia also makes me wish I could live there. But truth is, we really do live in Narnia.

This morning, as I rode my bike, fog piled up on far-off Rogue River. Mountains stretched beyond. Honking geese flew over my head, and meadowlark song drifted from the field beside me, holding the scent of wet grain. Staircasing clouds hugged Mount McLoughlin. An enormous beam of light shot through a group of clouds to the south. If I could reach that beam of light, it seemed I could step into another dimension.

The morning reminded me of another, long ago, when a rainbow fell in my lap.

I didn't even know such a thing could happen, but I looked it up afterward and discovered that, indeed, it can. Of course, I already knew it could, because I had experienced it.

Prospect, Oregon
Spring 2007

While I drove down a winding mountain road, a rainbow paralleled my path in the field beside me. I had never seen one that close before. I slowed my car while my eyes followed its track. When the road turned toward the rainbow, the inside of my car exploded with color.

I pulled to the side of the road in wonder.

Knowing my awesome Creator Redeemer had let me experience something extraordinary, I sought Him for the reason behind the gift. I didn't receive the answer then, but months later, during an inversion below Lost Creek Dam, another rainbow fell into my lap.

Seeing such a thing once made me sit up and listen. Seeing it twice awoke my soul that God is still very much in touch with His creation.

Rainbows are a promise from God. I viewed these rainbows as a special promise for me. Life would get hard, but God would be with me through it all. Not only that, but He also would bring good out of what seemed impossibly bad.

I've lived long enough to see the truth of that promise, and I'm still living it. Life has grown hard, but God's promises are true. I have experienced that truth.

Eagle Point, Oregon
2021

A friend of mine does not believe in my awesome Creator Redeemer. He is attempting to discover God through knowledge and intellect. I often have told Don that the only way he will really know God is to experience Him. When the eyes of his soul are awakened to see the spiritual realm, then the intellect will follow. Not the other way around. I pray daily for Don to experience my awesome Creator Redeemer.

Experiencing God takes faith. A letting go of intellect and gaining a mistrust of our own knowledge.

That statement may sound crazy. We have to use our intellect and knowledge to understand anything. Yet, the more I see Cat struggle with his words, and the more often I see him fall into confusion, the more I am convinced there is something beyond our brains that we can better trust.

Cat's brain betrays him these days. He feels absolutely certain things have taken place when they haven't. But, at the same time, he can give me insight into some of my most profound quandaries. Where does that knowledge come from?

I believe it comes from the heart of God. Cat's brain may betray him, but Holy Spirit remains true.

When we give up leaning on our own understanding and acknowledge God in all our ways, we discover truth that reaches beyond our understanding. We act out of soul strength instead of brain cells. This is what it means to die to self.

I once told my granddaughter, Rachel, that it appeared to me, she hadn't yet died to self. She was attending college at the time.

"That doesn't sound like something I want to do," she said.

I laughed, finding her honesty refreshing.

None of us want to die to ourselves. We have even bought into the lie that we cannot love others until we love ourselves. The Sacred Writings (Bible) never say that. The concept of dying to self is consistent throughout the New Testament. It's part of being born again.

Jesus explained the concept by talking about a kernel of wheat falling to the ground and dying before it could be planted and bring new life. In dying to self, letting go of preconceived notions, and stopping defending ourselves, we find true freedom. In this place of surrender, we give ourselves over fully to an utterly trustworthy Creator.

Revival is in the air. Catch it if you can.

China
1987

In 1987, when I first traveled to China, I set Psalm 139 to music. The words focus on how we cannot go anywhere beyond God's Spirit.

> *If I go up to the heavens, you are there;*
> *if I make my bed in the depths, you are there.*
> *If I rise on the wings of the dawn,*
> *if I settle on the far side of the sea,*
> *even there your hand will guide me,*
> *your right hand will hold me fast.*

Strolling along the walkway of West Lake in Hangzhou, China, I sang those words while playing guitar. A young man from the

East African country of Comoros walked beside me. I will call him Peter. We had been talking for quite a while, and I sensed he was on the verge of taking his life. His family had sent him to China to learn agriculture to save his people from famine. The pressure drove him to the edge.

I recognized the symptoms. Our son Rob's best friend had recently committed suicide.

I stopped. "We all feel pain."

He stopped. "But you are American? Surely, you do not suffer."

Chinese students crowded around, trying to hear our words and practice their English. The smell of cherry blossoms mingled with body heat. A guard stood on a drum not far away.

I had been in China for several weeks. With no contact home, I felt as if I had dropped into another century. I was terribly homesick.

Oh rats, I have to share Christ with this man. I'll probably go to prison and be here for a long time.

It was both illegal to congregate and proselytize.

"People throughout the whole world are undergoing the same kind of sufferings," I said, a loose translation of 1 Peter 5:9. Then I boldly raised my voice to a near shout. "But Jesus Christ came to set the captives free!"

Time seemed to stop. I saw everything in a freeze-frame.

My traveling companions, Julie Wheeler and Judi Zanitsch, looked stunned. They were wise to stay well enough away.

The guard still stood on the drum, looking for anything out of the ordinary. The crowd around us continued to gather. How big could it grow without the guard noticing?

But I also could see hope shining in Peter's eyes.

Still carrying my guitar, I started walking again.

Peter fell in beside me as the entire group of young people hovered around us. We were like a cloud moving on the ground.

"I'm going to tell you the words of God," I said, loud enough for Peter and the crowd to hear. "These are not my words. They are from the Bible; they are the words of God."

Peter nodded, his eyes solemn and searching.

I had memorized the entire book of 1 John before traveling to China, believing God would somehow use it. I was carrying God's Word in book form, but I also was taking it in conversation form. Knowing my own words may or may not do any good, I chose to share the Word of God. I knew it would not return void. God's Word is powerful and life-changing when the Holy Spirit is involved.

"That which was from the beginning," I started, "which we have heard, which we have seen with our eyes, which we have looked at and our hands have touched—this we proclaim concerning the Word of life. The life appeared; we have seen it and testify to it, and we proclaim to you the eternal life, which was with the Father and has appeared to us."

Peter listened intently, nodding in all the right places as I continued to verse nine. "If we confess our sins, he is faithful and just and will forgive us our sins and purify us from all unrighteousness."

Peter stopped and grabbed my arm. "That's what I want to do. I want to confess my sins!"

The crowd pushed against us now. Everyone wanted to be as close as they could. I sensed many of them wanted to confess their sins and accept Christ.

I stole a glance at the guard, who was looking the other way. I took Peter's arm and said, "Let's walk."

The cloud of young people continued to hover around us as we moved.

"We are going to pray," I said. "You can pray in all kinds of ways. You can kneel. You can stand up. You can lie flat on your face. Or you can just talk to God like we are going to do right now. You can repeat after me, or you can say it in your own words."

Peter nodded.

"Jesus," I said.

"Jesus."

"I have sinned just like everyone has, and I don't want to sin anymore. I know it hurts your heart."

Peter repeated the words.

"I know you sent Jesus to become one of us and to pay the price for my sins. Please forgive me and take away my sin. I renounce my old way of life. I turn to you as my Lord and Savior."

A murmuring broke through the crowd. Many students were praying right along with us.

"I trust you," I continued. "Thank you for loving me. Thank you for dying for me. Thank you for saving me from my sins."

Tears streamed down Peter's face as he repeated the words.

Tears washed other faces as well. One young woman's eyes shone as she looked toward Heaven.

"Today is the beginning of a new journey for you!" I said in a voice loud enough for the entire group to hear. It seemed to echo across the lake.

I spotted another guard standing on a different drum not far from us. He stared back at me with a look of awe on his face.

Had he heard the words? Had he prayed the prayer?

I won't know for sure until I reach Heaven.

I went on to share the rest of 1 John. I also shared the meaning of sin as rebelling against God and breaking His rules. "His rules are not hard," I said. "Our lives are better for following them. In fact, Jesus said that by loving God and loving others, we will keep all His rules.

The crowd dispersed, and my traveling companions and I took turns answering Peter's many questions. When I returned home to America, I sent him a French Bible in his language. He read the entire thing in a single month.

"Revival is in the air. Catch it if you can!"

Voices

The enemy of our souls is attacking the Word of God these days. It makes sense if you think about it. The Word of God is life to us. Without it, we have a difficulty discerning which voices to listen to. Voices speak around us all the time, easily sidetracking us.

When I lead my coaching class, I talk about how voices affect us. I illustrate this effect with a diagram of a bull's-eye target with four concentric rings.

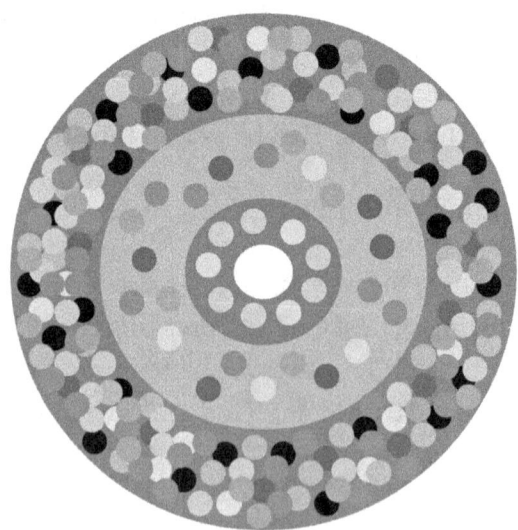

The Outer Ring

The outer ring teems with voices. It includes everything we hear every day of our lives—social media, TV, news, radio, podcasts, YouTube, friends, family, neighbors, books, magazines, songs. When we are focused on the outer ring, we also hear the voices from the inner rings, but they are all but drowned out in the cacophony.

A cacophony of voices demands our attention at any given time. Our attention is drawn in so many directions that we no longer know how to choose what is truth. We take a little bit of this idea and a little bit of that idea to form our personal beliefs. We rarely consider them long enough to know whether all our ideas actually work together or not.

While talking by phone, I once asked a granddaughter about her purpose in life.

"To be the best version of myself I can be," she said.

"So . . . who determines that?"

"Well, I do."

"You do?" I asked. Then I fell silent.

"Yes."

Pause.

Then she said, "But—"

Pause.

"If I do, then that means a serial killer determines what is the best version of themselves. Surely, that can't be right? But then—"

Pause.

"But I must be the one to determine what is the best version of me."

Pause.

"But then—"

She went back and forth for several more minutes. Then she said, "Oh, Grandma! You're making me think hard!"

We all need to think hard. Instead of sifting through all those thoughts and voices that bombard us on a regular basis, let's home in on the only voices that deserve our time.

We need to be aware of those voices in the outer ring, but we also need to let them stay on the outside. Let them be the noise they are and give them little heed.

The Second Ring

The second ring heading toward the middle of the target contains the voices of people who have caught our attention. We've read their books. We've studied their lives. We've taken part in their classes. Their words have proven to be true, and their lives mirror what they say. We won't do everything they suggest, but we will consider their opinions and weigh any decisions against other things we know. We usually keep fewer than twenty people in this ring.

The Third Ring

The third or inner ring is relegated to a few good friends and mentors or teachers who have earned the right to speak into our lives. These are either people you admire greatly or who know you well enough to realize where you should be cautious and where you can move ahead. After careful consideration, we usually do what these people suggest, but not always. Often, fewer than ten people populate this ring.

The Center Ring

The center ring or bull's-eye belongs to *One* who has earned the right to be heard at all times. Our Creator Redeemer knows everything about us. He knew us before we were born. He knows our thoughts before we think them. His thoughts about us outnumber the grains of the sand. When we hear His voice, we should obey at all costs. He knows what our hearts truly desire even better than we know ourselves.

In life, we generally start with that outer ring. World noise constantly bombards us. In truth, we should start with the inner ring or bull's-eye and move outward. After clearly hearing God's voice, those other voices will fall back into white noise where they belong until we no longer heed them at all.

Revival is in the air. And it starts with us!

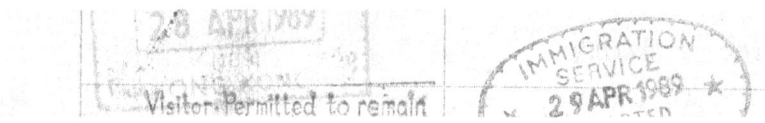

SECRET MISSION: AWAKENING YOUR SOUL

1. Is Christ is more important to you than He was when you first dedicated your life to Him? If so, write down in what ways. If not, ask God to show you what distractions need to go (such as busyness) and what needs to be added (such as quiet time in the Word of God).

2. When you listen for God's voice, do you hear Him clearly? If yes, write down the things He is showing you. If no, go to Him in prayer and ask Him to speak to you. Then set aside some daily time to read the Sacred Writings (Bible).

The Apostle John knew the need to drown out other voices and keep his soul awake to God. John walked and talked with Jesus and gave his life to the death for what he knew to be true. He immersed himself with the Word of God. He studied and made himself approved. Truth drowned out the noise of the world and gave John a purpose that extended beyond his time.

I love everything written by the apostle John in the Bible. He was the youngest of the disciples and lived the longest after seeing Jesus rise into Heaven. I would like to get back to the faith of the early church—a faith that carried them with great joy through troubled times. John's passion humbles me.

Christ enabled John to write about Him, talk about Him, and testify about Him; He enables me to do the same. I may not be able to see Christ in the same way that John did, but I can see His hand in the way He answers prayer. I'm aware of His presence as I live and move and have my being in Him.

I desire to take John's passion into my relationships. Yet life often gets in the way. We may not face persecution in America, but we tend to live our lives at a frantic pace. Too often, we don't begin our mornings asking God what we should do with our days. Our days are already full before we even begin.

A few years ago, I drove by an orchard, where someone had pulled old-growth pear trees out of the ground. The huge trees lay on their sides with their roots exposed to the air. Those trees bloomed on their sides, not knowing they were already dead and would never bear fruit. They provided a sad reminder of what our lives can easily fall into if we don't take time to gauge our spiritual health.

Those dead trees mean a lot to me. Back in 1990, the Lord gave me Psalm 92:12-15:

> *The righteous will flourish like a palm tree,*
> *they will grow like a cedar of Lebanon;*
> *planted in the house of the LORD,*
> *they will flourish in the courts of our God.*
> *They will still bear fruit in old age,*
> *they will stay fresh and green,*
> *proclaiming, "The Lord is upright;*
> *he is my Rock, and there is no wickedness in him."*

I have marked many dates beside that passage, as the Lord has repeatedly given it to me as a promise . . . 1990, 2002, 2003, 2004, 2007, 2013, 2017, 2019, 2020. I was once young, and now I am old. I'm constantly reminded of that fact since COVID-19 restrictions. Yet, I am still a green tree. I am bearing and will continue to bear fruit. I am a standing tree!

Like the apostle John, I want to live my life in such a way that whenever I sit down to write or speak about what God has done in my life, the language will pour out in a flow of ecstasy. We Secret Agents must awaken our souls every morning to tune into the One Voice above all others. In this way, we will continue to be nourished and growing—standing trees that still bear fruit.

Jeremy Cathcart.

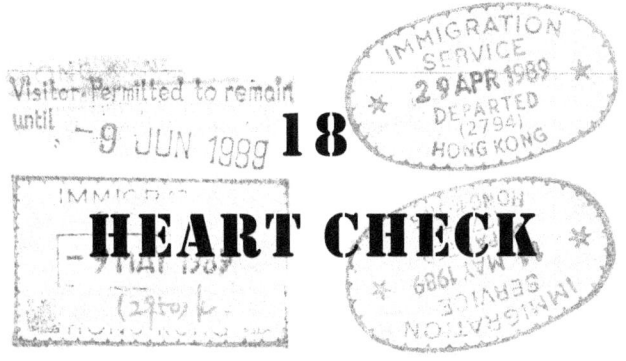

18
HEART CHECK

> If our hearts condemn us,
> we know that God is greater than our hearts,
> and he knows everything.
>
> —1 John 3:20

Eagle Point, Oregon
2021

CAT EXPERIENCED TWO SEIZURE EPISODES on January 9. He was totally unresponsive and shaking all over. Though it was the first occurrence in more than a year, he had several more seizures during the next few weeks. Each one seemed to take a small piece of him.

Our new normal terrified me. I should have been thankful for a year of grace. Instead, I stared at a future filled with pain. I feared losing my husband of nearly fifty years. I forgot that my awesome Creator Redeemer promised to walk through all the pain with both of us.

He'll be there for Cat, and He'll be there for me.

That realization was again tested in the early hours of Resurrection morning.

Eagle Point, Oregon
April 4, 2021
Easter

The call came in the middle of the night.

I scrambled for my phone. Caller ID let me know it was our daughter Michelle. I flew up and out of bed. Too fast. I had to lean back on the mattress to keep from falling to the floor.

The interruption was upsetting Cat, so I snuck into the kitchen. In the past, Cat would have been up with me, praying with me and offering comfort. Not so in our present circumstances dealing with dementia.

Michelle's hysterical sobs mingled with words I could not understand. Then one word stood out, "Jeremy."

Jeremy is Michelle's thirty-year-old son, our grandson. He's a larger-than-life young man who encourages nearly everyone he meets. He was a YouTube sensation as he traveled through Europe, training others how to ride and do tricks on a scooter. Jeremy never meets a stranger, and he often gives money and his favorite clothing to homeless people. He works hard, is a clean freak, and always smells good. He makes everyone around him feel special.

Heart Check

Years before, when Michelle's husband left her and her six kids, Jeremy stepped in to keep what was left of the family together. Always there for his mother, he talks with her every day.

Michelle's sobs continued amidst a garble of words. While waiting for a chance to speak, I strained to understand. I thought I heard the word "dead."

That couldn't be possible.

Jeremy had suffered from depression two years before, but lately, he had been doing well and had much to live for. He was in the finishing stage of building a tiny home and was planning to be the best man for his baby brother's wedding. We had been getting back to our much-relished conversations about God, who we both loved so much.

"Michelle," I said, "I can't understand you."

"Mo-o-o-o-om!" she wailed, and then the babble continued.

I still didn't understand what had happened. We were on the phone for a good twenty minutes before I knew my grandson was truly dead and that my daughter wanted to join him.

While Michelle continued to wail, my heart broke. Tears washed down my face. I turned to God in those long moments, searching for wisdom and strength and courage.

My daughter needed me, but she was a long-haul truck driver, thousands of miles away. I wished I could pull her through the phone line and hold her in my arms. "Where are you?"

"I don't kno-o-o-o-o-ow!"

She could have been in any one of forty-eight states. I hung up with a promise to call right back. Then I called her dispatcher and discovered Michelle was parked at a rest stop in Missouri. I found a nearby church, hoping to reach a counselor to go to her, but the website didn't provide a phone number.

Back when Michelle was still living at home, I was a women's counselor in the county jail. Many times, I woke in the middle of the night and dressed to go help someone in need. Our church number was available 24/7. I wondered briefly, how many other things had changed in the way Christians show love to one another.

Finally, I called the sheriff's department near her and reached a police dispatcher. Isaiah was kind and as compassionate as any church counselor, but he couldn't leave his post. We both agreed Michelle should not be driving. He called another deputy and arranged for him to help. But when I called Michelle back, she was already on the road, still sobbing.

I stayed up the rest of the night, reading Scriptures to her and talking her off the ledge of suicide. At first, I had no idea where to turn in the Bible, but through prayer, I found the Holy Spirit leading me to all the right verses.

Michelle and I both found some comfort. She made it to Georgia before she pulled over for a mandatory rest.

Jeremy was always the one to pick Michelle up from the airport. She didn't think she could handle not seeing him when she returned home, so she kept driving. After two days and two sleepless nights, Michelle parked the truck somewhere in the Southwest and returned home to Vancouver, Washington.

The Unseen Realm

The terrifying call about Jeremy's death came on Easter morning ... Resurrection morning.

Jeremy had been working on his car. The vehicle fell off the jack and crushed him. His body had been lying there for two days, but his spirit was immediately transported to the place we call Heaven.

We miss him here in this realm, but Jeremy does not miss us. I can see him laughing and dancing.

"You're going to love it here," he says to me with shining eyes. "There's so much color!"

How do I see and hear him?

I'm not exactly sure. But I know his words are more than imagination. More than just a knowing. More than a vision. It's the part of me that knows without being connected to the brain. It's the part of us that experiences all the senses when going through an out-of-body experience. It's the part of us that leaves the body upon death and will one day be reunited with our bodies in Resurrection.

I believe this is what Paul talks about in 2 Corinthians 4:18. He says, "So we fix our eyes not on what is seen, but on what is unseen, since what is seen is temporary, but what is unseen is eternal."

All the stuff will pass away. Everything will be made new.

Secret Agents walk increasingly less in the seen world and increasingly more in the unseen realm; because we know Resurrection is ahead of us.

The Power of Prayer

After receiving the news of Jeremy's death, and after all of our family had been informed, I asked my prayer warriors to pray for us. I've been doing this ever since a raging forest fire was racing for our country home years ago.

The Timber Rock Fire had doubled from ten thousand to twenty thousand acres overnight and was predicted to double again. Our home was not expected to survive. Caring friends had come to pack up our important belongings and carry them to safety. Cat and I stayed behind to keep water on our roof and the surrounding trees.

As I was getting ready to turn off my computer and pack it up, I thought about asking my friends to pray that the fire would turn in on itself. At first, it seemed a selfish thing. Others had greater needs than I.

But then, God whispered in my heart, *Do you want this answer to prayer or not?*

"I want it," I said aloud. I sent the email and packed up my computer.

That night the winds turned the other way.

Weeks later, the fire no longer threatened. I opened my computer and was surprised at how many people had answered my email. Their prayers had turned the fire!

Since then, I always ask for prayer when we are experiencing a specific need. Prayer changes things. And the prayer of a multitude shakes up both Heaven and Earth. At least that's the way it seems to me. Whenever I have asked for prayer, God does miraculous things, not always in the way I had hoped, but always in the *best* way. While I have a temporal view, He has an eternal view.

"Therefore we do not lose heart," Paul says in 2 Corinthians 4:16-17. "Though outwardly we are wasting away, yet inwardly we are being renewed day by day. For our light and momentary troubles are achieving for us an eternal glory that far outweighs them all."

As my friend, Ghostdancer Shadley, says, "Creator Yahweh is never a day late."

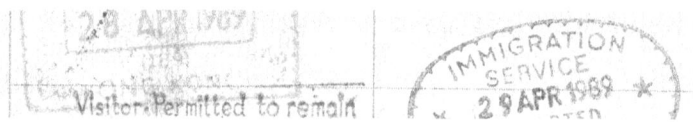

SECRET MISSION: CHECKING YOUR HEART

1. What are you feeling right now? (Hopeful, sad, confused, afraid, or . . .?) Take those feelings to your awesome Creator Redeemer. If you feel hopeful, thank Him. If you feel confused, ask for His wisdom and guidance. He is there for all who call upon Him.

2. This life (inside the realm of time) is the only opportunity we have to prove our loyalty and love to our faithful Creator. In what ways are you doing that?

Prayer Changes Things

Because of prayer, Cat and I decided not to travel to Vancouver for Jeremy's memorial—one of the most difficult decisions of my life.

Everything in me wanted to be with my daughter and grandchildren. I knew Cat couldn't handle a long trip or endure crowds. So, I tried to think of ways someone else could stay with Cat while I traveled.

During this time, my friend Erin Bader and her husband stopped by our home on their way back to Idaho. I shared my dilemma. The four of us joined hands while they prayed for us to have God's wisdom.

Later, when I asked Cat about attending the memorial, he was adamant that he could not make the trip.

"Are you okay with me going?"

He shook his head. "I need you here."

I went outside and sat in the warm sunshine, listening to birdsong and breathing in the scent of spring. All that beauty, yet tears streamed down my face. My life had changed in such a way that for the first time, I could not be there for my daughter. My husband needed me. After all the seizures, Cat required routine. Even Michelle's phone calls upset him so that I had to go outside or into another room to talk with her.

Because of the prayer that Erin and David had prayed over us, my tears were short-lived. I was soon able to trust God.

The peace lasted until the night before the memorial.

Michelle called me sobbing, "I feel like I've lost my son *and* my mother."

My throat constricted. I couldn't say a word.

Michelle apologized for making me cry and disconnected.

I began to make plans. I would buy a plane ticket and fly up to Vancouver and back in one day. It wouldn't be much different than running off to the grocery store. Surely, Cat would be fine.

I cried the rest of the day—not sobbing, but tears would not stop. That evening I fell into big choking sobs and had to hide in the bathroom. The pain was greater than anything I had felt before. I sobbed for all the loss . . . for Jeremy . . . for not being able to be there for my daughter . . . for feeling inadequate as Cat's wife in this time when he needed me most . . . for the loss of what we had shared for so long.

I was feeling the same emotions Michelle felt on that first horrible night of receiving the news of Jeremy's death.

Cat and I crawled into bed. I woke several times through the night. Each time, I found my pillow soaked with tears. I had never before wept while asleep.

Then I dreamed I had a baby. In my dream, Cat took that baby and slammed it to the ground. I woke up screaming, something I had never done in our fifty years together. I also found myself angry with Cat. "I should have made him go with me," I reasoned, or simply told him, "I'm going on my own."

Finally, I asked seven of my closest friends to pray for us.

Again, prayer made a difference.

I reminded myself that Cat could not help his reaction. He knew what he could or couldn't endure. He had been there for me for fifty years. Now, it was my time to be there for him.

When it came time to watch Jeremy's memorial service on Zoom, we watched it together. The service celebrated our grandson's life, and I could sense Jeremy smiling.

Heart Check

Jeremy dealt with some significant issues, even going to prison. Yet, he shared the love of Jesus with everyone he met.

Everyone.

"How's your heart?" Jeremy would always ask, even total strangers.

Someone might say, "No problem. Working out, low cholesterol. I'm fine."

"No, man," Jeremy would say. "I mean you and Jesus. How's your heart?"

That's a good question for all Secret Agents to ask themselves. "How's my heart? Am I trusting Jesus today more than yesterday? Am I expecting the unexpected at every turn?"

How's my heart?

Cat and Sandy.

19
CREATOR REDEEMER

> Now my beloved ones,
> I have saved these most important truths for last:
> Be supernaturally infused with strength
> through your life-union with the Lord Jesus.
> Stand victorious with the force of his explosive power
> flowing in and through you.
> —*Ephesians 6:10 (TPT)*

Art Du Jour Gallery, Medford, Oregon
2013

THE SUN WAS STILL BEATING DOWN on me when I noticed the time. I had five minutes to make it to the art show featuring my lions. I shut off the engine and climbed off the tractor, smelling like fresh-cut hay mingled with sweat. Leaving the tractor in the middle of a windrow, I sped to tell Cat I was going.

He was halfway down the upper field on the bailer.

"Gotta go!" I hollered.

He climbed off the bailer and kissed me. "You did a good job. Look at the windrows."

Where he pointed, magic light filtered through an inversion painting the entire field with a soft yellow glow. An attachment on my tractor had scooped up the hay into beautiful rows stretching for nearly a mile. Bushes and trees lined each end, and a creek ran down one side. Forrested hills surrounded us.

"I hate to leave the job unfinished," I said, "but my crowd awaits me."

We both laughed.

Most of the time, my "crowd" consisted of twenty to thirty people. But that was not the case this night. I arrived at the gallery to find nearly one hundred people waiting for the "lion artist." I had no idea the local newspaper had featured my colorful lions on a full-page spread. If I had known, I certainly would have arrived in better shape. Bits of hay still clung to my skirt.

The evening turned out to be one of my most special events. A local TV station interviewed me while I gave a painting demonstration. People from all walks of life praised my work. I treasured every bit of encouragement.

A small woman with piercing eyes pulled me aside. Tears glistened down her cheeks. "Tell me about your lions."

"They all reveal an aspect of our Creator Redeemer."

I pointed toward the wall that held fourteen of my favorite lions. "I start with the eyes, so the lion is looking at me the entire time I'm painting. It's as if I'm pulling him out of the canvas. By the time I've finished the painting, I know which aspect of Creator Redeemer's heart the lion is revealing."

She took a step back. "I can see why you call him Creator, but what is this Redeemer stuff?" She scrunched up her face. "I don't like that."

I smiled. "But your Creator is also your Redeemer. He wants to redeem every broken piece of our lives."

She shook her head violently. "I just don't like that." She pointed at one of my lions. "Tell me about this one," she said. He really speaks to me."

Her words didn't surprise me. Everyone who comes to my shows discovers one lion that seems to jump out at them. "That's *The One Who Sees*," I said. "He sees all the pain, all the hurt, everything you've ever been through, and He cares."

She clasped her hands across her heart. "O-o-o-o-oh. I can feel him looking into my very soul."

Tears streamed. She continued to tell me how my lion was reaching into all the hurt of her life. Then her eyes narrowed. "I don't like that Redeemer stuff. You should just call him Creator."

I laughed. "But He *is* your Redeemer. You can't separate one from the other. He created you, but He also wants to redeem you."

She stood, staring at the lion for nearly an hour while I talked with other art enthusiasts. Each pointed out their favorite lions. The woman never purchased the painting, even though it reached into her heart. She simply didn't want to admit that anything in her life might need redeeming. To admit that would mean that she needed a Redeemer. Trusting someone outside herself was more than she was ready to do.

I've prayed for her often since that night. I saw a broken woman in need of the love and redemption only her Creator Redeemer can give.

Colina de Luz, Mexico
Early 1980s

An orphanage is a place where it's easy to see our brokenness. Back in the eighties, I made several trips to Colina de Luz (Hill of Light) in La Gloria, Mexico. Sometimes I traveled with a group; other times I traveled alone. Around fifty children lived there during that time. I grew to love every one of them. I prayed for them, wrote letters throughout the year, and visited them whenever possible.

On this particular trip, I had traveled with a group. Our leader was planning for us to take all the kids to the beach in the afternoon. I was overlooked as I remained hidden in the kitchen. I scrubbed for hours at the inside of the oven, trying in vain to remove the crust hardened from years of neglect. Finally, after calling it done and stepping into the sunlight, I discovered the rest of my mission team had left for the beach without me.

No laughter, no children. Only the barking of dogs sounded from a nearby hillside.

Savoring the quiet moment, I breathed in the fresh scent of sea air blowing across the bare hills. Then I walked through the dormitory while praying for each child who would sleep in the bright quilt-covered beds that night. Looking through a window above one of the beds, I was surprised to see a young boy sitting alone in the playground sand. I wondered how he could have been overlooked by the beach crew.

I hurried outside and halted just inches from the lone boy.

His tiny balled-up fists rubbed his eyes with a controlled fierceness. He just kept rubbing, up and down, up and down.

Dropping to the sand beside him, I pulled him into my arms.

Still, the little fists kept on churning. No sobs escaped the boy's throat, and not even a tremble shook his rigid shoulders, just that incessant rubbing.

I prayed for God to show me what to do. Using the few Spanish words I knew, I attempted to soothe the boy. When the tiny fists never let up in their vigil, my tears dropped to the ground between us.

The laundry woman passed us on her way to the clothesline.

I was so excited to see another adult, I jumped up and frightened her in my enthusiasm. "Por favor," I said. "A little boy needs help."

She dropped her laundry basket on a concrete slab and marched over to address the boy in his native tongue.

He answered concisely, but still those little fists continued to rub.

"His name is Antonio," said the worker. "This is his first day here." Without another word, she returned to gathering the row of faded shirts off the line.

First day? And no one here to greet him . . . No substitute parent, no other children . . . just me?

I plopped on the ground next to Antonio and sobbed, feeling an overwhelming sense of inadequacy. I sent silent prayers to my Creator Redeemer asking for wisdom. After a few moments of unrestrained weeping, I felt little hands reaching around my neck. I looked down to see Antonio's dark eyes probing mine. I pulled him into my arms, wishing with all my heart I had something more to give him.

We were still clinging to one another when laughter rolled through the air. Fifty pairs of feet ran across the sand of the playground.

Antonio looked out at his new world with frightened eyes. Suddenly, a shadow fell over him. We looked up to discover Brett Meador, the youth pastor, standing over us.

"Hey, young man," Brett said. "I have a pair of boots here that don't seem to fit anybody. But these boys think you are the right size."

Three heads bobbed their approval while Antonio's eyes grew wide with surprise.

Brett reached down to unbuckle Antonio's sandals. Every boy held his breath while first socks were slipped over Antonio's feet and then the boots. A perfect fit!

Antonio screamed with delight and jumped up to dash across the playground. He twirled in circles and raced back and forth, seeing how fast the new boots would run. He danced around his three new friends and jumped over rocks. Then, one of the older boys slipped an arm across Antonio's shoulders and walked with him as though they were a couple of old buddies.

My gaze followed the two boys until they stood on the dormitory porch. Just before they entered the door, Antonio reached up to whisper into his new buddy's ear. Then, he turned and ran toward me, his face alight with wonder and newfound joy.

I stood, and he grabbed me in a hug that nearly toppled us both to the sand. Then he threw a bunch of Spanish words at me and ran off to catch his new friends.

I'll never forget those dancing boots.

How was it that Brett had saved one pair of boots that just happened to fit the feet of a little boy he had never met?

That's the Redeemer part of our Creator. He sees our brokenness, and He reaches out in ways we would never expect.

Once we have surrendered our lives to our awesome Creator Redeemer, we Secret Agents discover that He keeps His promise to never leave us or forsake us. He is with us wherever we go. He is in every place we are.

Box R Ranch, Southern Oregon
July 2018
Sacred Places

I have long been aware of sacred places—places where I sense the presence of God in a special way.

The first time I stepped foot on Box R Ranch, I knew I was standing in a sacred place. I looked out across the green pastures and breathed in the smell of mountain air. I had come home.

I didn't know then, back in the eighties, that I would one day live there in our little Jenny Creek cottage. In the meantime, I enjoyed many days at Box R Ranch, sometimes working with at-risk youth, other times meeting with my artist friends, and still other times booking a cabin for family gatherings.

I finished my book, *Wild Woman: A Daughter's Search for a Father's Love,* while staying in one of the cabins. On the last night, I sensed God telling me to pull on my shoes and go outside, as if someone had called my name. I discovered a herd of elk grazing in the glow of the setting sun. Their musky scent rose around me. When the last one disappeared into the forest, a bull elk began his bugle, a love song echoing through the forest and across the meadow.

Elk are one of my favorite animals. My Creator Redeemer had given me the experience as a special gift. He also gave us the most special gift of living on the backside of Box R Ranch. We moved to the Jenny Creek Cottage in 2013. It became one of the happiest times of our lives as we basked in the fairy-tale setting bordering the forest.

In July 2018, a raging fire came roaring toward our little valley. Plumes of a fire thunderstorm rose in the air south of us. Helicopters and firefighters filled the sacred meadow of Box R Ranch. I daily walked the land, praying for the fire to turn the other way and for the safety of the firefighters. I also reminded God that Box R Ranch was a sacred place, deserving protection.

One day, I climbed the mountain above our cabin to see if the fire was drawing near. We were on standby evacuation at the time. Everything important was packed in our horse trailer that sat in the relative safety of the sacred field at Box R Ranch. Many of our neighbors had fled to town. The most adventurous of us decided to stay. If the flames came too near, we planned to join together at the ranch. The meadow and pond would give us a defensible space.

I stood in a far-seeing place. Miles of forested mountains stretched between me and Mount Shasta, California, another sacred place. Flames engulfed much of that forest as I watched a Boride bomber passing through the cascading plumes.

Fear mingled with sadness in my heart. "Don't forget this is a sacred place," I whispered to God.

He whispered back. *Everywhere you walk is a sacred place.*

I straightened. Holy Spirit lived inside me. I was always in a sacred place!

At the time, I accepted the realization for what it was—a gift from Creator Redeemer, an acknowledgment of His presence and grace that is always with me, making every space a sacred place.

Our Creator Redeemer constantly offers us gifts such as this. The words of a song I wrote years ago say it best:

Do you recognize His smile in the sunrise across the land?
Do you know His touch when He heals you with His hand?
Do you know His truth to free you from all your worldly gain,
day after day?
Day after day, He calls you by name.
In the unexpected places and in unexpected ways,
day after day, He calls you by name.

Often, we Secret Agents miss the gift because we aren't expecting the unexpected.

Miami, Florida
1990

"Miami Airport, please." I jumped into the front seat of the taxi. "Hope you don't mind. I get sick riding in the back."

"That's okay," the driver answered.

I detected a familiar accent, reminding me of my trip to Siberia. "Where are you from?"

"Miami," he mumbled.

"Born and raised?"

He straightened his cap with one hand, "You are a nosy young woman."

"Nosy perhaps," I laughed, "but not so young. Your speech sounds Russian to me."

"My name is Boris," he said. Then he told the story of how he had left a good job in Russia to immigrate to America.

"It must have been difficult to leave all your engineering training behind you," I said.

"I wanted my children to have choices." He guided the taxi through a crowded intersection. "I came to America so they could have the best of what life has to offer. My son is a doctor, and my daughter recently finished college."

As I watched his fine hands working the steering wheel, I was struck by his willing sacrifice for the needs of his children. His selfless view of life was so much like that of Christ that I couldn't help but ask if he was a Christian.

"Oh no. I was raised an atheist. I can't even understand such things."

"But I think you can," I answered. "Because Jesus calls us His children and left His heavenly home for us. Surely you can understand that kind of love after all you've done for your family. Do you have a Bible?"

He confessed that someone had recently given him one, but it remained unopened because he didn't think he would be able to understand it. When he pulled the taxi to the curb of the Miami International Airport, I turned to him. "I'll make a deal with you," I said. There is a God in Heaven who has big dreams for His children, even bigger than you had for yours. You promise me that you will read your Bible, and I'll promise to pray for your understanding."

His solemn eyes held mine. "It's a deal."

"One more thing," I said. "Promise that you will think about God."

It didn't seem like much at the time, a simple conversation with a busy man in a harried town. But looking back on it, I think I gave him the best possible gift—an opportunity to consider an abundant life in Jesus. The finest preaching in all the world can't match the simple truth of the love found in the Gospel. Our Creator Redeemer gives us gifts, which in turn, we Secret Agents can give to others.

Stay Alert!

Years ago, when I was leading worship at Applegate Christian Fellowship, Pastor Jon Courson said:

> *The man or woman used by God*
> *will not devote unnecessary time to doing necessary things.*
> *They will streamline their life as much as possible*
> *because they realize the battle is raging,*
> *the time is short, the calling is great.*

I've never forgotten Jon's advice. The calling *is* great. The battle *is* raging. The time *is* short.

We all face difficult days and lonely nights. The book of Ephesians speaks of the battle we face and admonishes us to, "... be strong in the Lord and in his mighty power. Put on the full armor of God, so that you can take your stand against the devil's schemes. For our struggle is not against flesh and blood, but against the rulers, against the authorities, against the powers of this dark world and against the spiritual forces of evil in the heavenly realms" (Ephesians 6:10-12).

The passage goes on to encourage us to pray in the Spirit on all occasions with all kinds of prayers and requests. "... With this in mind, be alert and always keep on praying for all the Lord's people" (Ephesians 6:18).

It takes courage and grit to be alert. Secret Agents learn to endure and stay in the fight.

We fight against evil. The presence of evil is what has caused all the pain, all the sorrow, all the sickness, and all the death we endure. This is a spiritual battle that affects our very souls. Our Creator Redeemer promises an end to evil. This is our calling: Hold onto what we know of Christ and bring ourselves and others into His glorious light

We Secret Agents are not alone in this battle. We don't depend on our own strength, because explosive Holy Spirit power works in us.

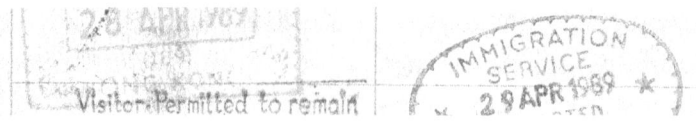

SECRET MISSION: REMEMBERING YOUR CREATOR REDEEMER

1. After asking God for guidance, list the ways He has touched your life. Nothing is too large or too small. Keep this list handy and add to it as God reveals things to you.

2. In what ways are you actively holding onto your faith?

Central Point, Oregon
Early 1980s
River Walk

One day long ago, Cat and I had a terrible argument. What caused the argument has escaped my memory. What resulted will forever be etched in my mind.

I walked out.

I didn't just walk out; I ran.

Cat had established specific rules for our marriage. We would never go to bed angry. We would always, no matter what, sleep together. And if I ever left, that would be the end of our marriage. Those rules saved our marriage more than once in those difficult years following the loss of our wilderness home. But on this day, I hit rock bottom.

Our family of seven found ourselves transplanted from our dream home in the forest to a crowded two-bedroom house in the middle of town. The crisis alone was enough to make or break our marriage, but the adjustment from country to city living nearly did us in.

Whenever I opened my front door to holler for the kids to come in for lunch, the echo resounded for blocks. In time, I learned it takes less volume to yell down a city street than it does across twenty acres.

Our children experienced their own problems. Coming from the country, they were tagged with names such as *goat ropers* and *hillbillies*. Our oldest son found a different way home from school every day to avoid the inevitable fistfight. Our youngest son dealt with the changes by turning into a whiner.

Yet through it all, Cat faced the biggest adjustment. The company he worked for went out of business. He found himself in the unemployment line facing day after day of rejection.

If I had been wise, I would have helped him through that rejection. Instead, I added to it.

I didn't feel Cat was reaching out to the kids enough. He didn't understand their problems, and he didn't understand mine. How could I feed a family of seven with so little money? We had no alone time. The boys shared one bedroom, the girls the other. Cat and I slept on a hide-a-bed in the living room. Every argument, and there were plenty of them, involved the entire family.

On this particular day, my rock-bottom day, I resorted to tears while Cat stood over me in our living room. I had just come back in after stepping between our oldest son and a neighborhood bully.

"You have to stay out of the middle of it," Cat said.

I looked up at him, ready to plead my case. I caught my breath, shocked at the anger in his eyes. Where had the love gone? The concern? What had happened to romance?

Some people talk about how their lives flash before them in a moment of facing death. That's what happened to me as I faced the death of our love. The long-ago months of courtship rolled before me like a newsreel running in my mind. When did Cat stop bringing me flowers? When was the last time he had taken me on a date? When was the last time he had invited me *anywhere*?

Suddenly, I needed out. I ran through the door and jumped in my car, peeling rubber in the street. I could barely see for the tears. Without a plan, I drove. Who could I turn to? Who would understand?

Cat was my best friend. If I couldn't turn to him—

At that moment, I realized I couldn't live without Cat, and I couldn't live with him.

I ended up on a dirt road overlooking the wild and scenic Rogue River. I planned to hurl myself into the water churning over Gold Ray Dam. As I stood there looking at that swirling water, I lost my nerve. What if I just got hurt and didn't die?

Creator Redeemer

I ran back to my car and sped farther down the river below the dam until I finally found a place to end my life. I slammed the car to a stop.

I jumped out and waded into the water, not caring if anyone saw my reckless act. The Rogue River was famous for claiming several victims every year. I walked out, wearing a dress and sandals, waiting for the roiling current to carry me away. I walked to the other side of the river, turned around, and returned.

No people witnessed my near-death experience. Few people visit here in the winter months.

Wet and shivering, I crawled into my car. When I returned home, I hid in our one bathroom. I stood under the shower's hot water, attempting to wash away all my confusion.

While I changed into dry clothes, one of our kids hollered, "Mom! What's for dinner?"

I laughed. No one seemed to notice I had been gone.

Years later, I confessed to Cat what I had done. On his side, he never said a word about my leaving. He broke his rule and forgave me.

That's the way it is with our Creator Redeemer. When we break His rules, He forgives us.

One time, I shared this story with a Native American friend, Laura Grabner, of the Warm Springs Tribe.

"That was your River Walk," she said.

I stared at her.

She held my gaze and continued. "God changed the river bottom and flow of water for you. Like He did when the children of Israel crossed the Jordan River."

Was it possible?

After talking with Laura, I returned to the river for the first time since the incident. I stood on the bank, breathing in the scent of wet earth while I stared at the raging water. Two riverboats were fighting their way through, rising and falling with each rapid. Everyone onboard wore a life vest.

At that moment, I absolutely knew there was no human way I could have crossed that section of river on foot. I never got wet above my waist, and my sandaled feet never stepped on one rock. I've been calling it my River Walk ever since.

The book of Joshua in the Sacred Writings (Bible) records the crossing of the Jordan in chapter three. A lot of people find it hard to believe this amazing story. I don't have any trouble, because I've experienced something similar.

Once Secret Agents experience Creator Redeemer in such a way, they are never the same.

Creator

From reading this book, you know that Cat and I are facing some difficult days. Cat keeps telling me our awesome Creator

Creator Redeemer

Redeemer is returning soon to take us home with Him. Followers of the Jesus Way call this event the Rapture. It does, indeed, seem quite possible that it may happen in my lifetime. If so, then we also can expect an amazing outpouring of the Holy Spirit . . . another Jesus Movement in full swing!

Because of that hope, I've been praying for God to give back Cat's words. Cat is speaking less and less these days.

In God's great mercy, He may do that very thing. He can still rewrite the stars.

But if He doesn't, I will still trust my Creator Redeemer, because He has proven Himself to be entirely trustworthy.

Most days, the fire of God keeps me going. Yet, some days I doubt. On those, days I wonder if God is really here. Each and every time I doubt, He speaks the same words to my soul:

WHO ARE YOU TO FORGET THE LORD YOUR MAKER?
THE MAKER OF HEAVEN AND EARTH!

Each time He speaks those words to me, I look up and see God's hand on the beautiful creation around me. I say aloud, "Oh yeah. An awesome Creator spoke all this into being. And before He spoke it, He thought it. He thinks; therefore I am."

Then I recall the enumerable things my Creator Redeemer has done in my life and the promises He has given for the future. He is in the details.

He is enough.

Sacramento, California
1958
Billy Graham Crusade,

When I was ten years old, Grandma Lela took Momma and me to a Billy Graham Crusade. I don't remember anything about the sermon, but I do remember the final song, "Just as I Am."

Music was my passion. I had already learned how to play the piano by making myself a paper keyboard and teaching myself the notes. Perhaps that's why I felt such a strong urge to go forward with hundreds of people heading down the stadium steps toward the platform. Thousands of voices were singing in harmony, the most beautiful sound I had ever heard.

I knew if I asked Momma, she would say no. So, I burst through the crowd and headed toward the field below. I was small enough to make my way through.

I followed the crowd into a large tent with wooden benches stretching throughout. I sat on one of the benches, and a counselor led me in a prayer to accept Jesus as my personal Savior. I wasn't sure what that meant. But for the first time, I knew I believed in God. I also didn't know what that meant. But I had heard and believed He was someone, or something, extraordinary who had created the earth and everything in it. And the stars, and the heavens, and everything in them. And everything beyond.

Grandma Lela had told me this, and I had seen how God changed her life. She didn't get angry all the time and no longer cursed. I loved my Grandma Lela. I wanted this God that Billy Graham had talked about and my Grandma Lela loved.

After I prayed with the counselor, I turned and saw my mother. Tears streamed down her face as she prayed with another counselor. Today, I look back and am amazed at how God used my escape as a way of getting my mother to come to Him. She was an introvert and would not have gone forward, except that she had to find her child.

The counselor who helped her find me in that sea of people also helped her find God.

Later, at home, Dad was furious. He hated the church and anything to do with it. After many tears and arguments, Momma decided she and I would attend church without Dad.

Though our church was small, Momma and I both grew in our love for God. Many gray-haired ladies took her under their wing, and I made friends with some of the other kids. Sunday nights were my favorite. We would sing song after song and could make requests.

One Sunday night is imprinted in my memory. We were singing the words of, "There Shall be Showers of Blessing."

> There shall be showers of blessing:
> This is the promise of love;
> There shall be seasons refreshing,
> Sent from the Savior above.

Suddenly, the window on the right side of the stage was flung open!

The pastor's wife screamed with surprise as bags of groceries were thrust through. A lady came over and led the pastor's wife to the window. As we kept singing . . .

> Showers of blessing,
> Showers of blessing we need;
> Mercy-drops round us are falling,
> But for the showers we plead.

. . . those bags just kept coming. The pastor's wife stood with her head in her hands, weeping with joy.

I'll never forget that night. It beautifully represented what showers of blessing can look like in real life. The showers had come from hearts full of love for the pastor's wife. That love had been placed there by a faithful, loving God.

Ezekiel 34:26 says, ". . . I will send down showers in season; there will be showers of blessing."

The great preacher, Charles H. Spurgeon, once said, "God will send all kinds of blessings. And all His blessings go together like links in a golden chain. If He gives you saving grace, he will also give you comforting grace. God will send 'showers of blessings.' Look up today, you who are dried and withered plants. Open your leaves and flowers and receive God's heavenly watering."

This is my mantra: Look up to God and His promise of love. I can count on His seasons of refreshing and for the comfort only He can give through these broken times. Surrendering my will to His leaves me open for the refreshing showers that will bring new life.

Redeeming Love, written by Francine Rivers, is one of my favorite novels. She based the story on the biblical book of Hosea. Toward the novel's end, there is a scene where Angel, the main character, returns to her husband. Naked with her arms flung wide, she runs into her redeemer's arms. Her nakedness is a symbol of complete surrender.

Back when I was a naked hippie and surrendered my life to the Creator and Redeemer of my soul, nothing else mattered. This Secret Agent will leave this world in just such a way, with arms opened wide for an eternal embrace.

We fly soon.

Jeff Bates and Sandy Cathcart leading worship with Matthew McCollum on drums.

THE SONG
(October 3, 2020)

I've been singing the Song all of my life.

It first came to me through tall timber and fields of grain
On frosty mornings and tree lined lanes
When I trekked across mountains, it whispered my name
I repeated the Song to Nipper, my dog and very best friend
Together we heard the Song on the wings of the wind

I believed in the Song.

It was part of my world
It comforted me when I was a young, lonely girl
When no one else was around
it taught me to believe
in something more than what my eyes could see

I sang the Song to all my animal friends
Knowing full well they understood what Creator intends
He would bring healing someday and make full amends

Then I lost the Song.

Through no fault of my own, circumstances carried me away
From quiet mountain valley to noisy array
I could no longer hear the Song
Over shouting accusations and growing pain

I lost my way, though I still tried to sing
But the Song came out as a mournful thing
A deep cry of my heart with no words to explain
The hurt and the loss, separation and pain

A river called.

I answered its plea
Stepping into the water, "Please, take me."
The river churned high
Cold up to my thigh

"No," the Song said. "This is not part of my plan."
Then an unseen staff struck the sand
I walked across completely unhurt
My feet planted firmly on solid dirt

The Song came through then, loud and clear
"Sing it again for all who can hear.
My love reaches out to far and near!"

I've been singing the Song all of my life.

The Song is a part of me, from before I was born
It opened creation on the very first morn
It breathed life into the depths of me
And into every living thing

*The Song is a part of Creator's heart
Even before He formed the very first part*

*The Song reaches out through all eternity
Looking for hearts that will truly believe
And sing each line in perfect harmony*

I've been singing the Song all of my life.

*I hear it now even on the blackest night
It's a Song of redemption, restoration and sight
A King will come with a shout and a fight
Doing away with all evil, sadness and pain
Restoring the mountain to peace once again*

*That's the way of the Song; it speaks to the heart
And those who attend will not miss one part
It's a place of beginnings, a place to embark
A place to look back and a place to look far
A place with a future, a hope, and a plan
For every woman, child, and man*

I've been singing the Song all of my life.

TAKE THE SECRET AGENT QUIZ

VISIT
www.scatsandycathcart.com/secretagentquiz

to discover
your SSA (Secret Agent Rating)

You will also receive a free gift of the

SECRET AGENT CODE

ACKNOWLEDGMENTS

Back in my early days of walking with Christ, I thought it was just Jesus and me.

In a sense, it was.

Bottom line, it's Jesus and me.

Yet, I have since realized that Jesus adopted us into a family. Relationships are what it's all about. First of all, our relationship with Jesus and His Father and His Holy Spirit. Then our relationship with the families He has blessed us with and our brothers and sisters in Christ. Then our relationship with the world.

Jesus said all the commandments are wrapped up in two: Love God and love others.

All the people mentioned in this book are a big part of my story, but so are many who are not mentioned. You know who you are. Everyone I've come in contact with has contributed to who I am.

One of my biggest blessings is the tribe God has now given this only child in the way of family. I love you all, and you are all a part of my story as I am a part of yours. Thank you for being in my life.

ABOUT THE AUTHOR

Sandy Cathcart is a freelance writer, photographer, and artist who paints under the name of SCAT. She has published several books and hundreds of articles and photos in national and regional magazines. Sandy and her husband, Cat (known as The Cat Man), worked as a cook and guide for 4E Guide and Supply, a wilderness outfitter, for more than a decade. She writes about Creator and everything wild.

The Cat Man and Sandy

Sandy has traveled extensively, fishing the Sea of Okhotsk in Far East Russia, sailing over Lake Baikal in Siberia, cycling the backroads of China, rowing across the rivers of Vietnam, swimming in Israel's Dead Sea and the Gulf of Mexico, trekking across Peru and Haiti, and hiking across Lantau Island. With The Cat Man, she has rafted rivers in inflatable kayaks, hunted deer and elk, skied cross-country and downhill, canoed marshlands, tracked antelope across the desert, fished rivers and lakes, sailboarded and water skied, climbed mountains, hiked daily, and just about anything else there is to do in the outdoors.

"Everywhere I walk is a sacred space," Sandy says, "because the Holy Spirit lives in me."

That mantra has carried Sandy's message of an awesome Creator Redeemer to everyone she meets. Today, she continues that message through every available means despite not being able to travel.

"I am still a green tree," Sandy says, "I can bear fruit until Jesus comes to get me. And you can too!"

CONTACT

www.scatsandycathcart.com

sandy@sandycathcartauthor.com

Reviews are like gold to authors.
If you have enjoyed this book,
please consider leaving a review
on
Amazon,
Goodreads,
or
share on your
favorite social media.

Thanks so much!